THE BEST
FOR
OUR KIDS:
Exemplary Elementary Guidance & Counseling Programs

Martin Gerstein

Marilyn Lichtman

A division of the American Association
for Counseling and Development
5999 Stevenson Avenue, Alexandria, VA 22304

The American School Counselor Association, a division of the American Association for Counseling and Development
5999 Stevenson Avenue
Alexandria, VA 22304

Cover and text illustrations by Margaret Scott
Cover design by Sarah Jane Valdez

Library of Congress Cataloging-in-Publication Data

Gerstein, Martin
    The best for our kids : exemplary elementary guidance and counseling programs / Martin Gerstein, Marilyn Lichtman.
        p.   cm.
    Includes bibliographical references.
    ISBN 1-55620-066-8
    1. Personnel service in elementary education—United States—Case studies.   I. Lichtman, Marilyn. II. American School Counselor Association. III. Title.
    LB1027.5.G444   1989
    372.14—dc20   89-36853

CONTENTS

FOREWORD

The co-authors of this book, Martin Gerstein and Marilyn Lichtman, have done an outstanding job in compiling discerning information about exemplary elementary guidance and counseling programs throughout the country. Readers should find this book useful in providing examples of what can work to enhance the learning environments for students in our nation's schools and provide our students with a sense of self-worth and direction for a positive future.

Elementary counseling programs should be an integral part of a kindergarten through 12th-grade comprehensive, developmental guidance and counseling curriculum. We still need to spread the word and communicate the positive effects that elementary counseling programs can have in our schools. At this point, we are working toward a goal of having elementary guidance and counseling programs in all of the nation's schools, run by professionally qualified and certified elementary school counselors.

As a secondary counselor, I am often frustrated trying to work with a student with a problem that has been festering for many years. Intervention at an earlier age, or the benefit of having been a part of a comprehensive, developmental guidance and counseling program in elementary school, could have made a positive difference in that student's life.

The point has been made repeatedly that problems that have been evolving over many years are well represented in our mental health and correctional institutions. I feel that elementary counselors, if given the opportunity to provide developmental programs, can assist in identifying the individual strengths and resources to prevent, intervene in, and remediate many of the individual and societal maturation and growth challenges that we face.

Active membership participation in local, state, and national professional associations that work to promote the improvement of school guidance and counseling is encouraged as a base of support and information for school counselors. Elementary counselors can be the foundation of the entire developmental guidance and counseling program that we espouse.

Elementary school counselors are in a position to have a positive impact on society by appropriately enhancing the potential, dignity, worth, and uniqueness of each student at an early, critical age. Exemplary programs described on the pages that follow will strengthen that opportunity for positive impact.

—Jim Whitledge
President
American School Counselor Association

PREFACE

This book is a product of a research effort to identify exemplary elementary school guidance and counseling programs and practices across the United States. Almost 200 separate programs were nominated from around the nation for their exemplary qualities. Each is listed in the appendix. Program descriptions from the 134 programs in 40 states, Puerto Rico, and the District of Columbia that responded to our call for information are included in the text. The 10 programs highlighted at a conference held in May 1988 are described in greater detail.

This book will enable counselors and other guidance workers to learn about the best practices in the field of comprehensive developmental elementary school guidance and counseling. Readers are encouraged to network with the counselors identified herein to share ideas and activities that work well in the field.

This publication is divided into four sections. Section 1 gives the background of how programs were identified and selected. Section 2 provides a detailed account of how 10 exemplary programs were chosen from those nominated. Program descriptions and sample activities are presented and the address and telephone number of a contact person is given. Section 3 includes information on the remainder of the programs. This information is categorized and summarized into several domains that represent the major emphases of elementary counseling and guidance. The final section describes how this research effort was evaluated and draws several conclusions about the future of developmental elementary school counseling. Current references and additional resources intended to help counselors who are beginning new programs as well as those who are seeking new ideas are included at the end of the book. The appendix will help the reader to network and to gain a better understanding of how this research was conducted.

ACKNOWLEDGMENTS

We wish to thank Shirley Woodall, 1988 Christa McAuliffe Research Fellow, for her contributions to this endeavor. Shirley was the kind of student every graduate school advisor admires—a self-starting, hard working, reliable, quick study. We trusted her to take care of the details and she never let us down. She will make an exceptional elementary school counselor and we wish her the very best.

Shirley Woodall was a member of the New River Valley Consortium for Elementary School Counseling. This consortium included teachers nominated by their school districts to train for positions as elementary school counselors. These young women and men were employed in seven school divisions in southwest Virginia. They gave generously of their time, energy, and considerable talents in the development of this project. Each was enrolled in a course designed to teach research methods for elementary counselors and each participated in one or more aspects of the activities described in this document. A heartfelt thank-you to:

Pam Chitwood	Pulaski County Schools
Carol Cox	Floyd County Schools
Charlene Doss	Pulaski County Schools
Vic Edwards	Giles County Schools
Ann Ferrell	Montgomery County Schools
Trudy Golding	Carroll County Schools
Beverly Haun	Pulaski County Schools
Susan Hood	Montgomery County Schools
Linda Jessee	Carroll County Schools
Karen Jones	Montgomery County Schools
Terry Kimbleton	Pulaski County Schools
Ann Laing	Wythe County Schools
Jeff McCoy	Pulaski County Schools
Janet Morgan	Wythe County Schools
Donna Surratt	Carroll County Schools

Patti Talbot   Montgomery County Schools
Ruth Vordo   Pulaski County Schools
Charlotte Williamson   Craig County Schools

We also wish to thank Norman Gysbers, Chairman of the ASCA publications committee, and the ASCA leadership, particularly President Jim Whitledge, for their support and encouragement in developing this book.

ABOUT THE AUTHORS

Martin Gerstein is an associate professor of counselor education at Virginia Polytechnic Institute and State University. He teaches graduate courses in counseling theory and techniques, counseling of special populations, and career development across the life span. He has directed two innovative programs to prepare teachers to become elementary school counselors in Virginia. Earlier he was the director of pupil personnel services in an elementary school district in southern California, where he implemented a developmental elementary school guidance and counseling program.

Marilyn Lichtman is an associate professor of educational research and evaluation at Virginia Polytechnic Institute and State University. She teaches graduate courses in statistics, research design, survey research, and qualitative methodology. She works closely with doctoral students in counseling and marriage and family therapy. Dr. Lichtman has directed various surveys and program evaluations of guidance and counseling programs at federal, state, and local levels.

The authors co-directed the conference on exemplary programs and practices in elementary school counseling held at Virginia Tech in May 1988. This book is an outgrowth of that conference.

SECTION ONE

A LOOK AT ELEMENTARY COUNSELING

Guidance began in the United States at the turn of the 20th century under the term *vocational guidance* (Gysbers & Henderson, 1988). Preparation for work with a primary focus on job selection and placement highlighted the efforts of the early guidance pioneers in the public schools.

Although elementary counselors were employed as early as 1910 in the Boston schools, there was a 50-year gestation period before the birth of developmental elementary school guidance in the mid-1960s. Faust (1968) described this gestation period by dividing it into three parts:

1900–1940s	The traditionalist period
1950–1965	The neotraditionalist period
1965–forward	The developmentalist period

In the traditionalist period, methods and techniques were borrowed almost exclusively from secondary school guidance practice. By 1950, however, elementary guidance began to change and a neotraditionalist model appeared. It emphasized a group counseling and learning climate in the classroom and consequently deemphasized traditional secondary school practices. This was in keeping with the focus on personal adjustment built around the counselor-clinical-service model Gysbers and Henderson (1988) described.

In the middle 1960s, the developmentalist period emerged. According to Faust, elementary school counselors began to stress individual and group work activities that were developmental and geared to all children as opposed to remedial and crisis-centered interventions for the few. Support for this developmental model in elementary school counseling can be found in the work of Dinkmeyer (1966), who described pertinent child development research that supported a developmental perspective, and Shaw and Tuel (1966), who developed an early model of a guidance program designed to serve all students.

In the late 1960s and early 1970s, we witnessed a clearer delineation of the developmentalist approach of Faust. Guidance was defined in developmental-comprehensive-outcome terms, with substantial support coming from leadership efforts of a number of state departments of education that developed guidelines for implementing developmental concepts into the public school curriculum with goals, objectives, and activities. This curriculum was for all students and was arranged sequentially, K–12. Concurrently, individual school districts, alone or in partnership with university counselor education programs, continued to study and delineate guidance program models. By the end of the decade a number of viable models of comprehensive guidance programs were available in the literature. The interested reader is referred to Gysbers and Henderson (1988, pp. 22–28) for a fascinating description of the accountability movement and the consequent emergence of developmental programs during this period.

The American School Counselor Association (ASCA) was organized in 1952 and became a division of the American Personnel and Guidance Association in January 1953. School counselors across the nation at that time numbered about 8,000, a number that grew rapidly. The ASCA journal began publication in 1953, and *Elementary School Guidance and Counseling*, a quarterly publication concerned with enhancing the role of the elementary, middle school, and junior high school counselor first appeared in 1966. Today it is an important vehicle for communicating practical information on program development and accountability, techniques for individual and small group counseling, classroom guidance activities, and implications from relevant research studies to the practitioner. ASCA has had a vice president for elementary schools in the governance structure since 1969, and ASCA has developed an elementary school counselor role statement (1974, 1981) in support of comprehensive developmental elementary school guidance and counseling for all children.

In the late 1970s and early to middle 1980s, efforts to mandate comprehensive developmental guidance programs in the public schools were initiated. The Commonwealth of Virginia mandated elementary school counseling at a counselor/student ratio of 1/500 (Gerstein, 1989; Hoffman, 1989), and elementary school counselors were also mandated in the states of Maine and West Virginia. Although the exact status of legislation for counseling programs and counselor mandates in all the states was not determined for this study, the conference described in the following pages drew responses from 44 states, the District of Columbia, and Puerto Rico in a call for nominations describing exemplary programs in elementary school counseling. Approximately 200 programs in the public school districts of the nation were nominated. It is evident, therefore, that elementary school counseling is a force in almost 90% of the states of the nation. It is likely that elementary guidance programs exist in some school districts in every state.

Today we are poised on the threshold of the last decade of this century. Publications are appearing to help school counseling and guidance personnel put the ideas of comprehensive developmental guidance into practice and to implement them on a results or competency-based framework. Books, reports, and guides that are recommended readings on the above topics are identified in the reference section. Additional information is listed in the Additional Resources and References section.

BACKGROUND

This background information was prepared by Shirley I. Woodall, a Christa McAuliffe research fellow in 1987–88. Ms. Woodall received a master's degree with a major in elementary guidance and counseling in June 1988 from Virginia Tech.

The Christa McAuliffe Fellowship Program is funded by the U.S. Department of Education. The program was established to provide grants to teachers for the development of innovative projects or programs, to enable and encourage them to continue their education, and to engage in research or other educational activities to improve the knowledge and skills of teachers and the education of students. The first grants under this program were awarded in September 1987. One hundred fifteen teachers from across the United States were selected to receive fellowships from the $2 million program that honors the late Sharon Christa McAuliffe, the New Hampshire teacher who died with other astronauts on the space shuttle Challenger in January 1986.

Shirley Woodall, an elementary school counselor in the Craig County, Virginia, public schools was then a graduate student in counseling at Virginia Tech. She received one of the first McAuliffe grants for a research proposal to identify exemplary elementary school guidance and counseling programs and practices across the United States, conduct a conference to showcase several outstanding programs, and describe the features of these exemplary programs for school counselors. The Virginia Tech counselor education department in the College of Education co-sponsored the project. Martin Gerstein and Marilyn Lichtman, both professors at Virginia Tech, served as project director and director of research, respectively.

Because of the Virginia mandate requiring all elementary schools to implement elementary school counseling programs by the 1989–90 school year, this project was timely for education in the Commonwealth. The conference afforded the opportunity for counselors, prospective counselors, supervisors, principals, and other educators to find out how successful elementary counseling programs are able to succeed. Participants also were able to learn the components of outstanding programs, discover innovative and effective practices, and discuss program implementation and evaluation.

The conference was held at the Donaldson Brown Continuing Education Center on the Virginia Tech campus in Blacksburg, Virginia, on May 12 and 13, 1988. Robert Myrick of the University of Florida was the conference keynote speaker. He is a nationally acclaimed authority on elementary school counseling and has written and spoken extensively on the subject. He is also a consultant to many school districts that are beginning new elementary school counseling programs. Myrick's focus was on what elementary school guidance and counseling can do for a school. He provided guidelines and suggestions on how a school district can establish a quality counseling program.

Libby Hoffman, currently a Virginia Tech professor of counselor education, was at the time of the conference the supervisor of elementary school guidance and counseling for the Virginia Department of Education. Hoffman has been at the forefront of the elementary school counseling movement in the Commonwealth for 10 years. She was instrumental in providing the leadership that resulted in a mandate to include counseling in all elementary schools in the state. She spoke to conference participants about perspectives on elementary school counseling in Virginia.

Kathleen Nininger, elementary school counselor, and Martha Blount, principal, at Back Creek and Bent Mountain Elementary Schools in Roanoke County, Virginia, presented a counselor/principal dialogue on the complementary roles of the elementary school counselor and the elementary school principal. Nininger and Blount have worked together and established a highly effective and successful program that is an invaluable asset to their schools and community.

Ten programs were highlighted at the conference. They represent some of the best elementary counseling programs in the country. The selection process used to identify these programs is described in the following pages. Representatives from these 10 exemplary programs presented information to the conference participants. These sessions covered a wide range of topics and unique activities, some of which are included in the program descriptions presented in section 2 of this book. There was a heavy focus on small group counseling and classroom guidance activities, with good representation from the other major components of developmental elementary school counseling, including individual counseling, consultation, coordination, and program evaluation. The conference was intensive and packed with information. More than 400 participants attended from Virginia and across the nation.

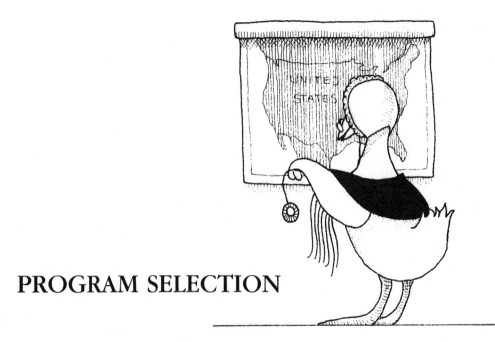

PROGRAM SELECTION

One of the primary goals of this project was to identify elementary guidance and counseling programs that were considered exemplary. We recognized that many excellent guidance programs aimed at the elementary level were already in existence. We wanted to identify some of these in order to recognize their efforts and share their expertise and experiences with those who were about to become counselors at the elementary school level, who were already practicing counselors, or who were counselor supervisors. Representatives of the selected programs were invited to give a presentation at the conference held at Virginia Tech. We also wanted to compile a list of exemplary programs in operation across the nation and help counselors develop a network for communication and sharing of experiences and ideas.

It fell to us, then, to develop a plan to identify exemplary counseling programs. We considered a variety of ways to locate good programs. One way was to examine the research literature to find out what others had done. Although this approach would yield some good programs, we feared that the details of how programs operated and the activities used in such programs might not be described thoroughly in the research literature. We also felt that we might miss many good programs, in part because the average elementary counselor is a practitioner and does not frequently contribute to the research literature.

A second way to locate good programs was to call upon the judgment and knowledge of experts. A third approach was to gather knowledge at conferences. Still another was to seek nominations from those considered knowledgeable. Although any one of these approaches would provide us with knowledge about some programs, taken individually they too might be limited in scope and miss some of the very best programs around the country.

We decided to combine elements of the several ways and use those in a research technique known as the Delphi approach to identify exemplary elementary guidance and counseling programs. The details of how we went about this process follow.

PROCEDURES

Step One—The Initial Pool. The first step in the identification process was to determine the initial pool of possible elementary guidance and counseling programs. We knew that we could not obtain a list of all elementary school counseling programs and that we probably would not want to work with such a massive amount of material. We decided to try to get a first cut at a list by answering the following questions.

1. *Could we identify the sources of information about elementary guidance and counseling programs?* Other than lists of the schools themselves, there is no readily identifiable list of all guidance programs. So we needed to find an alternate way to generate a list of programs to be included in the initial pool.

2. *How could we identify programs when no common list existed?* Because there is no readily identifiable list of guidance programs, we went about identification through an alternate route. We decided to identify categories of individuals who might have direct knowledge of guidance programs. We were interested in obtaining a broad range of programs that would be representative of all 50 states. Categories of individuals who would have knowledge of such programs included:

- **State supervisors of guidance** in each of the 50 states, Puerto Rico, and the District of Columbia. A list was obtained from the American Association for Counseling and Development.
- **Professors** at universities where training programs in elementary guidance and counseling exist. Hollis and Wantz (1986) served as a resource to identify this group.
- **The leadership of professional organizations** who might have knowledge of such programs. We went to the American School Counselor Association, the Association of Counseling and Development, the National Education Association, and the National Association of Elementary School Principals.

- **Editors** of journals that publish articles of interest to the elementary school counselor. These included *Elementary School Guidance and Counseling, The School Counselor* and *The Journal of Counseling and Development.*
- **Directors** of pupil personnel, directors of guidance, and supervisors of guidance in local school districts throughout the country. We chose those most visible in the profession through their writing and professional activities.

3. *How could we find out about these programs?* We contacted the individuals we identified in step 2 of this procedure and asked them to complete a one-page nomination form if they had any programs they wished to nominate. In addition to demographic data, we asked respondents to identify the primary focus of the nominated program and to describe briefly or list its strengths and exemplary features. We felt this would encourage people in the field to respond. The nomination form is reproduced in the appendix as Figure 1.

Step Two—More Information. The second step in the identification process was to obtain more information about the various programs that had been nominated. We received more than 200 nominating forms. This enabled us to contact representatives of the nominated programs directly for more information in order to make a more informed judgment about each program. We asked ourselves the following questions.

1. *How could we learn more about each program?* Some of the nominations we received provided detailed information about program content, activities, and format. Others were more general. We decided to develop a questionnaire that would be sent directly to a contact person in each nominated program.

2. *How could we go about designing a questionnaire that would get the information we wanted?* We wanted to get a variety of information about each nominated program. This included demographic information about the school or district, its students and the counselor or counselors, and programmatic information about activities, materials, and evaluation procedures. The questionnaire we developed had both closed and open-ended questions.

There were 10 open-ended items that asked people to respond to inquiries about the primary objectives, the major strengths and exemplary features, innovative or unusual practices, and any other unusual feature of the elementary guidance program. This format permitted considerable detail in describing certain features of each program. We kept the questionnaire sufficiently short to encourage individuals to respond. It was also easier for us to review a short questionnaire. A copy of the complete questionnaire, entitled "Exemplary Elementary Programs and Practices Questionnaire," is found in the appendix as Figure 2. The questionnaire was pilot tested on a group of 25 counselors in training. Their comments and suggestions were used to revise items. The appendix copy is the final version.

3. *Would nominated programs respond to a request for additional information?* We received more than 200 nominations. Some programs were nominated by more than one person. After adjusting for these duplications, we sent the questionnaire to 183 programs and asked that responses be returned within 3 weeks. Contact persons who did not respond were contacted again and encouraged to participate in the research.

Step Three—Narrowing It Down and Picking the Presenters. We planned to use information about every program in this publication. But it was clear that we would be unable to invite representatives from 183 nominated programs to give a presentation at a conference. A decision was made to select 10 programs that would be representative. This is where we used the Delphi technique. These are the questions that were raised.

1. *Who would be qualified to participate in the Delphi panel and rank the programs?* One critical factor in selecting exemplary programs was to identify a panel of experts to provide a broad representation of persons in a position to make informed judgments about elementary guidance and counseling programs. We did not want to limit our panel to individuals with a special perspective (e.g., university professors, state department supervisors of guidance, or school counselors). We wanted our panelists to include people in the field who were working as school counselors, others who supervised school counselors, those involved in the training of school counselors, and individuals who used school counseling services. To the extent possible, we wanted our panelists to be geographically dispersed.

With these conditions in mind, we went about identifying categories of individuals and the persons who might provide the representation sought. Because we estimated that 2 to 4 hours would be needed to complete the ratings task, we needed panel members who were willing to participate and also had the time to do so.

Fourteen panel members were selected, representing eight different categories of individuals knowledgeable about the field of elementary guidance and counseling. The categories included:

- Counselor educators (n = 3)
- Elementary school counselors (n = 2)

- Elementary school principals (n = 2)
- State department of education supervisors of guidance (n = 2)
- Counseling association leader (n = 1)
- Counselor education researcher (n = 1)
- Professional consultant (n = 1)
- Parent nominated by national PTA (n = 1)
- Elementary school counselor in training (n = 1)

The selection committee members and their affiliation are presented in the abstracted conference program that appears in the appendix as Figure 3.

2. *What is the Delphi technique?* The Delphi technique is a process to help a group of people reach consensus or convergence about given topics, issues, goals, or programs. Originally developed by the RAND Corporation to get a consensus about urgent defense problems without face-to-face discussion, it has been used widely since RAND's original work (Uhl, 1971). It is based on the idea that in order for each person's view to be heard and not be unduly influenced by group members who might be dominant or might exert group pressure to conform, members are not asked to come together for a face-to-face discussion and vote. Instead each person is asked to provide his or her input without meeting with other group members.

The next step is to inform each member of a Delphi panel of the combined or average vote of all panel members. Uhl (1971) referred to this as controlled opinion feedback. Panelists are then asked to revise any of their ratings if they desire to do so.

In a traditional Delphi approach, panelists are asked to identify issues, goals, or programs for consideration. We used a modified Delphi technique with the following steps.

1. We identified elementary guidance and counseling programs. All nominated programs for which completed questionnaires were returned to us by the due date were included. This included 101 of the 183 programs for which completed questionnaires were returned.

2. We provided questionnaires on programs completed by a representative of the program and a rating form to panel members. A copy of a rating form is found in the appendix as Figure 4. It is entitled "First Round Rating Form." Due to the large number of completed questionnaires, the responses were randomly divided into two groups with either 50 or 51 so as not to create an undue burden for some panel members. Nine panel members rated half the programs and four panel members rated all the programs. One panel member was unable to participate at the last minute because of a schedule conflict. All information that would identify a pro-

gram was removed from each questionnaire before the materials were sent to each panelist. Code numbers were assigned to the programs before sending them for review and rating. This resulted in an anonymous review, thereby removing any potential bias a given panel member might have for or against a particular program.

3. Each panelist received the following instructions. Using a four-point Likert scale of Strongly Agree (1), Agree (2), Disagree (3), or Strongly Disagree (4), rate each program (by number) for this statement: This program is among the best of this group of programs in terms of objectives, strengths, exemplary features, and innovative, unusual, or highly effective practices.

4. Average ratings were then calculated for each coded program, and a revised rating form that indicated the average rating for each program was sent to each panel member. This form appears in the appendix as Figure 5. The panel's instructions were to examine the average ratings for each program. They were then to compare their individual ratings with the average ratings. If they wished to do so, they revised their ratings and returned the form with the new ratings.

5. New averages were calculated based on the revised ratings. Programs were then placed in rank order. In order to have geographic representation, we decided that we would not select more than one program from any state to participate in the conference. With this as a guideline, we selected 10 programs that had the highest scores and invited their representatives to participate. All were able to accept.

FINDINGS

Several hundred individuals including state supervisors of guidance, professors of counselor education, directors of pupil personnel services, leaders in professional organizations, journal editors, and other knowledgeable persons were invited to nominate programs that were, in their opinion, exemplary. After eliminating duplications, we wound up with 183 nominations of elementary guidance programs from 44 states, the District of Columbia, and Puerto Rico.

Questionnaires describing 101 programs were received by the deadline. Five were incomplete or illegible and could not be rated. An additional 38 responses were received after the deadline. We included them in the follow-up analysis of the data. This represents a 73% response rate for the programs that were nominated.

Summaries of the ratings are provided in Table 1.1. After the first round of ratings, 33.4% of the programs received a rating between 1 and 1.9,

TABLE 1.1

Round One and Final Average Ratings of Nominated Programs.

	Average (Round One)		Average (Final)	
	Frequency	%	Frequency	%
1.0–1.4	11	11.5	11	11.5
1.5–1.9	21	21.9	26	27.1
2.0–2.4	35	36.5	26	27.1
2.5–2.9	16	16.7	14	14.6
3.0–3.4	10	10.4	14	14.6
3.5–4.0	3	3.1	5	5.2

indicating that the panel members *strongly agreed* with the statement that "This program is among the best of this group of programs in terms of objectives, strengths, exemplary features, and innovative, unusual, or highly effective practices." Fifty-three percent of the programs received a rating between 2 and 2.9, indicating that the panel members *agreed* with the statement that the program "is among the best of this group." Only 13.5% of the programs received a rating between 3 and 4. Such a rating would indicate that the raters *disagreed* or *strongly disagreed* with the statement that the program "is among the best of this group."

At the end of the second and final round of ratings, 38.6% of the programs received a rating between 1 and 1.9, 41.7% received a rating between 2 and 2.9, and 19.8% received a rating between 3 and 4.

Because one of the purposes of the Delphi technique is to try to achieve consensus, we might expect changes to occur between the first and second ratings, reflecting, at least in part, movement of individuals toward the average. However, our results showed that 32.3% of the ratings moved in the direction of agreement about quality of programs whereas lower ratings were given to 38.5% of programs (i.e., individuals moved in the direction of disagreement about quality of programs); and no change in the direction of rating was reported for 29.2% of the programs.

One factor that might influence results of such a procedure is reliability of ratings of individual raters between the first and second ratings. Table 1.2 reports these results. Little change overall was noted in average ratings between the first and second rounds. The overall average rating in the first round was 2.27 and the overall average rating in the second and final round was 2.24. In general, those raters who rated higher than average on the first round (in the direction of strongly agree) scaled their ratings

TABLE 1.2

Average Ratings of Panel Members, Round One and Final Ratings

Panel Member*	Round One	Final	Change
D	1.77	1.86	–
M	1.84	2.09	–
G	1.94	2.20	–
B	2.02	1.96	+
L	2.28	2.18	+
I	2.29	2.29	—
A	2.30	2.17	+
H	2.33	2.29	+
K	2.39	2.31	+
J	2.52	2.47	+
E	2.53	2.24	+
C	2.58	2.60	–
F	2.67	2.47	+
Total Average	2.27	2.24	+

*Reports data for 13 panel members. One panel member was unable to complete ratings.

down on the final round. Conversely, all those raters except one who rated lower than average on the first round (in the direction of strongly disagree) scaled their ratings up on the final round.

CONCLUSIONS

We used the procedures described above to identify exemplary elementary counseling programs in the United States. We sought *broad representation* of programs and used knowledgeable individuals to help identify them. We sought *objectivity* in selecting programs that were innovative and exemplary. Therefore, we used a Delphi procedure and a panel of experts on whose judgment we could rely.

The conference that was held attempted to meet the needs of a variety of people involved in the implementation of developmental elementary school guidance and counseling programs. The highly positive results of the evaluation discussed in section 4 indicate that the conference was a success.

In trying to determine what good developmental elementary school counseling programs do to help children succeed in school, we believe we were true to the ideal that Christa McAuliffe has come to represent.

The name Christa McAuliffe evokes images of the exemplary in educational ideas and methods. Helping children to become successful in school and to reach their greatest potential in life is the focus of developmental elementary school counseling. This project identified outstanding programs that are assisting children in reaching these goals. We believe Christa would have been proud that developmental elementary school counseling is being recognized as an effective, preventive measure that is a vital part of any outstanding educational program.

SECTION TWO

THE BEST
OF THE BEST

Section 1 provided a detailed account of how 10 exemplary programs were identified from the approximately 200 elementary guidance and counseling programs nominated. In this section, we will describe these 10 programs in detail. Figure 3 includes an abstract of each of these programs.

A representative from each nominated program was asked to complete a questionnaire and to send supporting materials. The descriptions of the programs discussed below are based on these questionnaires and supporting documents. We had to rely on the information sent to us (in almost all cases printed materials) for program descriptions.

These programs represent 10 different states: Arkansas, Florida, Indiana, Louisiana, Massachusetts, Minnesota, South Carolina, Texas, Virginia, and Wisconsin. Most of the programs represented are in suburban school districts. Two programs are located in predominantly urban areas and two programs are described as serving urban, suburban, and rural school districts. Only one program is located in a totally rural community. None of the 10 selected programs are in large communities having inner cities.

Five of the programs are located in communities where the student population is described as predominantly White. One program serves a predominantly Black population. Two contain substantial minority populations (over one third) and two contain significant minority populations (over 15%). By far most of the students are from middle-class families. Only one of the programs serves students of working-class families.

The programs have at least two common elements. All are described as being developmental in nature and provide services to all students in a preventive model. All are currently funded under regular district funds, although a few of them had been started with money obtained from grants or from other special funding.

The first four programs we will describe are districtwide programs. Most of them have been in place for quite a long time. As such, they are likely to have a philosophy, a structure, support services, and a plan for evaluation. In addition, because information was received from the district level rather than the school level, we often learned about fewer specific activities in the written material provided.

The elementary guidance program in the East Baton Rouge, Louisiana, school district is directed by Betty Addison, the Supervisor of Elementary Guidance. The program serves a predominantly Black, middle-class community. This district has developed numerous activities in the guidance program. We have chosen, in this description, to highlight those that can be used with parents.

The second program described is in San Antonio, Texas. Patricia Henderson is the Director of Guidance there. It began as a pilot project in the mid-60s and has grown to a comprehensive program, serving 30 elementary schools and schools at the middle and high school level as well. You should enjoy reading a sample of a task analysis that has been developed to help elementary school counselors in planning group guidance activities. The one we've chosen to highlight is based on distinguishing *what* you are going to teach from *how* you are going to teach it.

The elementary counseling and guidance program in Roanoke County, Virginia, is the third program described. Gary Kelly coordinates this program. This long-term program utilizes frequent evaluation to improve its guidance and counseling efforts. An interesting activity we have chosen to include is based on helping children recognize similarities and differences between themselves and others.

The fourth districtwide program described is in Eau Claire, Wisconsin. Jim Jacobs leads this effort. Like the others, this program emphasizes developmental classroom guidance. It describes the roles and responsibilities of counselors, and clearly spells out the program goals.

The remaining programs included in this section are located in a single school within a district and are operated by one counselor. Much of the strength of these programs seems to be in the dedication, knowledge, and skills of individual counselors. Their initiative, their drive, and their love of children may be the guiding force in their development of elementary guidance and counseling programs that have been judged as exemplary.

Wynne Intermediate School in Wynne, Arkansas, is a rural school serving a working-class community. Sue Hull is the counselor. Her leadership and initiative have helped this program to continue to remain of such high quality. This is the only one among the 10 programs that serves children in grades 3, 4, and 5 exclusively. You will enjoy reading about the Student Host Program this counselor developed.

Pinar Elementary School in Orlando, Florida, is located in a mixed community that serves an urban, suburban, and rural student body. The counselor at Pinar, Nancy Allen, has been there for 10 years and has developed many activities that she shared with us. We have described several in some detail.

Crichfield Elementary School is in La Porte, Indiana. The school serves students in grades K through 8. One of the unique features about this program is some large group guidance activities developed by the counselor, Sally Mayes. We have singled out an activity she calls "Wearing of Attitude Glasses" that we expect you will enjoy reading. It should be easily adapted to most situations in which discussions of attitudes toward self and others are important.

The Fort River Elementary School is located in Amherst, Massachusetts, a district with only four elementary schools. Mary Bradford Ivey utilizes a conceptual developmental model that we have described in some detail. Her delineation of specific counselor functions and activities should be especially helpful as you look at your own guidance program.

Located in Rochester, Minnesota, the Jefferson Elementary School program is the only one of its kind in the school district. This program is less than 5 years old and came about because of a guidance committee effort. Jane Bogan, the counselor, and Kathy Estry, chair of the guidance committee, spent considerable time looking at existing research, curriculum guides, and documents on guidance and counseling. A thoughtful resource guide has been developed so that a counselor can gain access to some of the most effective materials.

The guidance program at Forest Lake Elementary School in Columbia, South Carolina, is the last of the single school programs to be described in this section. Like all the other counselors who run successful elementary guidance programs, Ron Miles is actively involved in working in developmental classroom guidance activities. He makes a point of visiting all students and classrooms on a regular basis.

The 10 programs we have described were identified as exemplary by a jury of professionals in the field. They are illustrative of the excellent practices that reflect current thinking about guidance and counseling at the elementary level. Developmental classroom guidance seems to be the watchword. Addressing the needs of the whole child in the areas of education and learning, personal and social growth, and career exploration is evident. Serving as consultants to teachers and other professional staff and interacting with parents and others in the larger school community is a counselor goal as well.

Should you wish any additional information about the programs described, we have included an address and telephone number for each of these guidance leaders. They will be happy to work with you. Because a purpose of this publication is to encourage you to network, we also call your attention to the directory of almost 200 exemplary programs included in the appendix.

East Baton Rouge Louisiana

Background

East Baton Rouge Parish School District, Baton Rouge, Louisiana, serves 59,000 students in grades K through 12. This district represents a combination of urban, suburban, and rural settings in a 271-square-mile area. The racial/ethnic background of the students is predominantly Black and the socioeconomic status is predominantly middle class.

The counselor/student ratio is approximately 1 to 440. Certification and 3 years of successful classroom teaching are required of all elementary school counselors. The school division provides regular inservice education for counselors. To accommodate this, state law provides tuition exemption for counselors. Three major universities are located in the Baton Rouge area.

This program receives primary financial support from the regular district budget. Other school district support services include child welfare and attendance, alcohol and drug prevention teams, student appraisal, and school nurse services. Counselors also work closely with many community agency services including special placement for children removed from home, mental health, family counseling, programs for displaced home-makers, legal aid, food bank, programs for battered women, and psychological testing through the universities.

Brief Program Description

The elementary school counseling program in Baton Rouge is developmental and preventive in scope. Crisis intervention is secondary. Its primary focus is directed toward activities and techniques used with all students. These include instruction in decision-making skills, developing a healthy self-image and sense of responsibility, and the pursuit of academic achievement and personal development. All elementary school students participate in a counseling activity at least once each week.

Activities

This counseling program has developed many materials and techniques. Although many excellent and varied materials are used in this program, we will describe some *activities used with parents* in the Baton Rouge school guidance and counseling program.

1. Positive communication with parents is pursued in a variety of ways. One example is a letter sent home to parents that introduces counselors and provides some key ideas of what a counselor is and does.

An illustrated pamphlet sent to all parents inviting them to come and meet the school counselor is another example of how this district works on positive communication. Its simple, straightforward format appeals to parents of varied backgrounds. In keeping with other materials this school division has developed, it stresses the positive nature of counselor/parent communications.

WHAT IS A COUNSELOR?

A counselor is someone who listens no matter what you say.

A counselor is someone you can talk to when you feel confused.

A counselor is someone you can talk to when you need to share something very special.

A counselor is someone you can talk to when you feel angry.

A counselor is someone you can talk to when you feel worried.

A counselor is someone you can talk to when you feel proud.

A counselor is someone you can talk to when you feel frightened.

A counselor is someone you can talk to when you feel sad.

A counselor is someone you can talk to when you feel lonely.

A counselor is someone who is always a friend!!!

Parents:

Your school counselor is Mary Jones. Please feel free to call me at any time concerning your child. My telephone number is 555-1111.

---

2. A *Happygram* is sent to parents to indicate a child's outstanding achievement in character, participation in class, politeness, regular class attendance, and many other desirable behaviors. This serves to set a positive tone in counselor/parent communication. Students whose parents receive a *Happygram* are entered in a "student of the month" program. U.S. savings bonds are awarded at the end of each school term as part of an incentive program.

3. Another type of material used is a simple pamphlet for parents that describes the counseling program in a particular elementary school. The content defines elementary school counseling, indicates who may seek help from counselors, outlines specific tasks elementary school counselors perform, describes how an elementary counselor helps students, parents, and teachers, and indicates how a student may get to see a counselor.

4. Suggestion lists are provided for parents. These are prepared in some of the elementary school curricular areas as well as by level. For example, at the *preschool* level they include such suggestions as:

- Read to your child
- Discuss experiences
- Play word, letter, and card games
- Take your child to the library with you
- Keep a good supply of picture books
- Encourage your child to recognize signs and symbols in everyday life

At the *primary* level they include such suggestions as:

- Have your child read out loud to you and show interest
- Write down your child's experiences as told to you—a dictation game
- Play games with rhyming words
- Find words that begin and end with the same sound
- Use headlines and subheads in newspapers as reading sources

5. Additional printed materials have been developed for parents that stress a positive self-image:

HOW TO KEEP YOUR CHILD'S SELF-IMAGE STRONG

- Say something positive to your child each day.

- Try to see that your child achieves success in some way each day by offering a variety of activities.

- Give your child recognition for the effort he or she makes even though it may not come up to expectations.

- Make your child feel that he or she belongs.

- Listen to your child and look the child in the eyes when he or she is talking.

- Answer your child's questions openly, honestly, and immediately if possible.

- Do not embarrass your child, especially in front of others; do not make the child question his or her worth.

- Compliment the child when possible on creative ideas, improvement in performing tasks, etc.

- Encourage your child to be proud of his or her name, ideas, and work.

- Do not set goals so high that the chance of failure prevents your child from trying.

- Emphasize what your child does right instead of what your child does wrong.

- Treat your child as you would like to be treated.

6. In addition to printed materials and parent/counselor conferences, this district sponsors "Workshops for Parents." One recent workshop focused on getting involved with children's learning experiences. Presenters included teachers, parents, principals, representatives from family counseling services or the state department of education, the district supervisor of parental involvement, a VISTA volunteer, and the PTA president. Topics included such areas as parenting and child protection, helping a child to excel in school, and interpreting and utilizing school records.

7. A *Guidance Newsletter* is sent to parents of elementary school children periodically. A recent newsletter included the following:

RECIPE FOR A HAPPY HOME

Take 4 cups of love and 2 cups of loyalty; mix thoroughly with 4 quarts of faith. Blend in 2 spoons of tenderness, kindness, and understanding. Add 1 cup of friendship and 5 spoons of hope. Sprinkle abundantly with 1 barrel of laughter. Bake with sunshine and forgiveness. Serve generous helpings daily. (Serves entire family.)

Evaluation

Each elementary school counselor develops a written annual plan to provide a basis for evaluation. Components of the plan include annual goals, operational strategies, and activities to accomplish each goal by grade level. These are negotiated with the building principal before the start of the school year and reviewed annually to ensure that the program goals are being achieved.

Contact

Betty Addison
Supervisor of Elementary Guidance
East Baton Rouge Parish School District
P.O. Box 2950
Baton Rouge, LA 70821
(504) 922-5443

San Antonio Texas

Background

The Northside Independent School District in San Antonio, Texas, was one of two selected by the Texas Education Agency in 1965 to help determine what elementary school guidance should consist of in the Texas public schools. The pilot project demonstrated that a developmental program with one counselor per elementary school could produce measurable improvement in attendance, test results, and discipline, among other positive achievements. Today this comprehensive guidance program is in effect in 30 elementary schools, 9 middle schools, 6 high schools, and 2 special secondary schools of this rather large school district.

The elementary school counselor/student ratio is 1 to 489. The school division is located in a suburban community, primarily middle class. The racial/ethnic background of the district is White (50%), with a substantial Hispanic population (44%).

Brief Program Description

The primary objectives of the elementary school counseling program in the Northside Independent School District are, in priority order, (1) developmental classroom guidance, (2) responsive services, including small group preventive counseling, individual remedial counseling, and staff and parent consultation, (3) individual planning in the career and educational domains, and (4) system support offered to other programs on behalf of children and that offered to improve the guidance program.

The counselors in this school district work as team members with teachers and other campus-based specialists, with a pupil appraisal center staff that includes school psychologists and educational diagnosticians.

Major strengths of this program include solid district support (both political and financial) and a counselor performance improvement system that is reflected in the performance evaluation, supervision, and job description of each counselor.

Innovative practices in the Northside Independent School District include the development of two separate model guidance curriculum guides, a position paper on a comprehensive guidance program framework, and a guide to a counselor performance improvement system. Each of these publications can be purchased at a modest cost from the school district.

Activities

The Northside Independent School District offers a highly structured, districtwide developmental guidance program. All counselors function in the four priority areas noted in the brief description above. Each function has been assigned a percentage factor in the counselor's job description. Guidance curriculum receives 40%, individual planning and responsive services each take 25%, and system support the remaining 10% of the counselor's work time.

An example of how this is implemented in a typical school follows.

1. *Guidance curriculum.* Each classroom group benefits from a developmental guidance lesson each week. All counselors have been trained in the Madeline Hunter instructional technology model to assist them in offering classroom guidance.

2. *Individual planning.* Because the elementary school operates on a prekindergarten through grade five organization, individual planning is done with fifth graders to make a successful transition to middle school. This includes individual counseling sessions as well as guidance lessons and planning activities with each child. Children in grades 2–5 are helped to understand their standardized test results and to set educational achievement goals.

3. *Responsive services.* Small group counseling is provided for academically unsuccessful students at each elementary school. Special topic groups are offered as well. These are based on identified student needs. Brief family interventions are provided for parents and students. Creative methods to help parents improve their skills are used.

4. *System support.* There is a strong effort to reduce paperwork in this system. Counselors also meet monthly in geographic clusters to share ideas and reduce feelings of isolation for those who are the only counselors at a small school.

A task analysis format has been developed to assist elementary school counselors in the planning of group guidance activities and lessons. For example, in putting together a lesson, one first needs to know "what" one is going to teach before determining "how" to teach it. The "what" involves a series of steps outlined in the example below.

TASK ANALYSIS (WHAT YOU'RE GOING TO TEACH)

1. *Select terminal objective*

   Children will specifically label the feelings they are having in counselor-given situations.

2. *Brainstorm en route learnings*

   - What feelings are

   - Feelings are different than thoughts

   - What causes feelings
     good feelings: happy, caring, loving, affection, joy, glee
        (children need to know feeling words)
     bad feelings: sad, mad, anger, fear, depression,
        disappointment

   - Appropriate ways to express feelings, ways people express feelings

3. *Weed out nonessentials to the terminal objective*

4. *Ask diagnostic questions*

  • What age group is this?

  • What do they already know? Differences between thoughts and feelings; some global feeling words

  • What are they capable of learning? Capable of identifying some characteristics that describe feelings inside themselves; aren't capable of conceptualizing psychiatric definitions of big words

  • What feelings do they experience? Frustration, annoyance, anxiety, glee, joy

  • How much time do I have?

5. *Select sequence best for learning—order subparts*

  • Know labels—"good" and "bad"
    "good" = happy, caring, loving, affection, joy
    "bad" = sad, mad, anger, fear, depression

  • Know how characteristics of different feelings feel to themselves; how feelings feel "inside"; subtle differences; strength/depth of different feelings

  • Know how to analyze feelings in self or in a situation

6. *Identify unfamiliar or specially used terms*

  For your kids, you'd need to list the words appropriate to their age level and specify the "characteristics" they'll be able to identify with.

THEN—ON TO LESSON DESIGN
(HOW YOU'RE GOING TO TEACH THE ABOVE)
  Focus;
  Explanation;
  Practice; and
  Closure.

Evaluation

The Northside Independent School District Guidance Program is not static. A program self-study is completed at the end of each year, and the priority of various program components is modified according to the outcome of the self-study. Because each individual school staff sets guidance program improvement goals that are monitored and evaluated by the principal and the director of guidance, these individual school-level goals are incorporated into the district program design process. The model used for beginning this evaluation procedure includes a series of questions that have been developed by Norman Gysbers and Patricia Henderson in their 1988 book, *Developing and Managing Your School Guidance Program*, published by the American Association for Counseling and Development (AACD).

- Which program component should have priority for the counselors?

- Of the competencies that students need to learn, which should be emphasized at each grade level or grade grouping?

- Who will be served and with what priority: all students in a developmental mode or some students in a remedial services mode? And, what are the relationships between services to students and services to the adults in the students' lives?

- What domains will describe the scope of the guidance program and what competencies and outcomes will have priority?

- What skills will be utilized by the school counselors: teaching, guiding, counseling, consulting, testing, record keeping, coordinating, and/or disseminating information, and with what priority?

- What school levels will benefit and to what extent from the resources appropriated to the program: elementary, middle/junior high and/or high school?

- What is the relationship between the guidance program and staff and the other educational programs and staff? Is the sole purpose of guidance to support the instructional program? Does guidance have an identity and responsibilities of its own? Should it be a program or a set of services?

Contact

Patricia Henderson
Director of Guidance and Counseling
Northside Independent School District
5900 Evers Road
San Antonio, TX 78238
(512) 647-2218

Roanoke County Virginia

Background

The guidance program of the Roanoke County Public Schools in Virginia is a large, well-implemented program balanced in its components and clearly reflects the Virginia developmental model. The program is periodically evaluated, well supervised, and serves as a model for other programs being developed to meet a recent mandate for elementary counseling in this state.

The Roanoke County Schools Division consists of 17 elementary schools and 10 secondary schools. At the elementary level the counselor/student ratio is 1 to 423. The community served is suburban, primarily middle class, and predominantly White. Primary financial support for the program comes from the regular district budget. It has been in operation for 15 years, although the mandate for elementary school counseling in Virginia is very recent.

Brief Program Description

The primary objective of the elementary counseling program in Roanoke County is to assist students in such areas as the development of a realistic self-concept and self-direction, self and group awareness, capacity

31

for effective interpersonal relationships, effective communication skills, decision-making skills, and coping behaviors; to assist students in academic areas; and to develop wholesome attitudes toward the world of work. A major strength of the program is its long-term consistency in all schools of the community and the low turnover rate of staff. The Roanoke County school division usually does not split counselors between schools and works to match the counselor's personality with the school community carefully.

Other important features of this guidance program include a parent guidance committee in every school, and a peer counseling program in which selected high school students are trained in communication skills by elementary counselors and work in group guidance settings with fourth- and fifth-grade students. A highly effective practice of this districtwide guidance program is the commitment to staff development through in-service meetings for counselors on current and timely issues such as the latest research on school readiness or a review of programs for suicide prevention.

The team approach is used to help meet program goals. Other personnel involved on the team as needed are the school psychologist, speech pathologist, school nurse, visiting or homebound teacher, coordinator of gifted and special education, guidance and testing supervisors, and reading specialists.

Special materials have been developed for use in this program. The REACH manual was developed by the counseling staff. It ties in the objectives of the program with stages in the counseling process to ensure a systematic approach to guidance and counseling. A booklet describing the developmental characteristics of children has been prepared for use by parents. A PLUS manual has been developed for use in the peer counseling program. These materials are available at a modest cost from the Roanoke Area Counselors Association, P.O. Box 13145, Roanoke, VA 24031.

Activities

Activities counselors use in this program are not randomly selected; rather counselors develop them to meet specific developmental needs of students. In keeping with the developmental focus of the program, activities are always assigned to a specific grade level. Furthermore, they are tied to a specific objective of the counseling program as well as a Standard of Learning guidance objective of the Commonwealth of Virginia.

A sample of the activity "People Tags" provided below was designed by a counselor to meet a state Standard of Learning that emphasizes recognition of the similarities and differences between self and others and appropriate modes of interacting with others on an individual or group basis. The activity is further designed to meet the initial stages of the counseling process: establishing rapport and awareness and exploration.

PEOPLE TAGS

Description: An activity employing the "tag" idea to help children become aware of similarities and differences among individuals.

Materials: Three tags for each child. Tags can be cut from tag board and punched for stringing. Pens or magic markers used for labeling. Yarn or string for stringing tags. Timer. Activity length: 30–45 minutes.

Objectives:

- To help each child identify components that make him/her an individual

- To help children recognize similarities that make them each a part of the group

- To help children realize that though they are different from each other, they are still part of the group

How to conduct this activity:

Discuss purpose of dog tags for pets and service personnel. Stress identification of individual. Children then talk about "people tags." After the children are grouped in threes, they are given the following directions.

1. First tag will tell WHO I AM. Give each group 4 minutes to complete the tag for each group member that tells who they are (what they think, personality, looks, likes and dislikes). Use timer to limit group.
2. Second tag tells HOW I AM ALIKE. Set timer for 4 minutes. Tag completed for each member that tells how everyone in group is alike (e.g., looks, values, feelings, family, likes and dislikes).
3. Third tag is HOW I AM DIFFERENT. Similar to number 2, but looking at ways in which members of group are different.
4. Discuss how first tag was done alone, whereas tags 2 and 3 needed group working together.

Evaluation

The Roanoke County elementary school guidance and counseling program has been evaluated at various intervals since its inception. Initial evaluation took place during the first 2 years of the program and was continued at regular intervals until 1985. The process used was a pre- and posttest design to determine the effect counselors had on student achievement, self-esteem, and personal and social adjustment.

A second evaluation took place in response to a group of parents who were concerned with the philosophical basis of the program. As a result, a mental health committee of the county council PTA evaluated the program during the 1979–80 school year by means of an opinion survey that was distributed to all teachers and a randomly selected group of parents in each elementary school. This effort was in addition to the evaluation design described in the paragraph above.

A third type of evaluation occurred during the spring of 1987. The goal of this evaluation study was to determine if the elementary school guidance and counseling program was effective and to identify additional student needs. Group interviews, questionnaires, and individual interviews were conducted with counselors, teachers, principals, students, and parents.

The results of each evaluation effort since the inception of the program in 1973 indicate that the Roanoke elementary school guidance and counseling program has been a positive influence on children and parents who utilize the service.

Contact

Gary L. Kelly
Supervisor of Guidance and Curriculum Coordination
Roanoke County Public Schools
526 College Avenue
Salem, VA 24153
(703) 387-6416

Eau Claire, Wisconsin

Background

The Eau Claire, Wisconsin, School District was nominated because of its focus on developmental classroom guidance. It has been identified by the state of Wisconsin as a model elementary school program. The Eau Claire Area School District Elementary Guidance and Counseling Program began in 1974 with funds from The Elementary and Secondary Education Act of 1965 (Title III, E.S.E.A.). The program has grown from the original staff of two counselors to its present staff of eight full-time and four part-time counselors. It is funded through the regular district budget. The counseling staff serves 20 elementary schools ranging in size from 138 to 550 students. The average counselor/student ratio is 1 to 536. The counseling staff is supervised by the Assistant Director of Special Services, who coordinates the continued development of the program.

Eau Claire is geographically spread out over 200 square miles. The community is mostly urban, with some rural character. Socioeconomic status is primarily middle and working class and the racial background of the community is predominantly White.

Brief Program Description

This guidance and counseling program accepts the premise that counseling is the art of helping people. It subscribes to the philosophy of the

American Association for Counseling and Development that professional counselors are trained to share knowledge and skills with those who need help; that effective counseling is preventive; and that counselors help persons with their personal, social, career, and educational development.

This program utilizes principles developed by Robert Myrick of the Counselor Education Department at the University of Florida. We quote these important principles so that others may learn from them.

Developmental guidance

- is for all students;

- has an organized and planned curriculum;

- is sequential and flexible;

- is an integrated part of the total educational process;

- involves all school personnel;

- helps students learn more effectively and efficiently; and

- includes counselors who provide specialized counseling services and interventions

This program has defined the roles and responsibilities of school counselors along more than a dozen dimensions. It also clearly spells out its goals. Five of the goals are oriented toward students. They stress understanding and feeling positively about oneself; setting goals and making decisions; understanding career development; dealing with people; and understanding the importance of education and community resources. Goals related to assisting school personnel and parents also have been articulated.

One important strength of this guidance program is that student competencies along the dimensions of learning, personal/social, and career development also have been specified. An example of a competency in each of the areas is included here. For learning, the Eau Claire guidance program has written one learning competency as: Understand the school environment and what it expects of its students. In the area of personal/ social, an example of one competency is: Exhibit conflict-resolution skills with adults and peers. A competency in the career development area is: Acquire knowledge about different occupations and changing male/female roles.

Activities

In addition to programs in developmental classroom guidance, individual and small group counseling, consultation to educators and parents, and communication and public relations, the Eau Claire Guidance and Counseling Program has developed a number of innovative programs and activities. A partial listing follows. It is suggested that the reader contact the school district directly for information on how to obtain copies of these materials.

INNOVATIVE PROGRAMS AND ACTIVITIES

1. *Doorways and Windows: A Look at Children, Concern, Caring and Counseling* is a slide/tape presentation that explains the role of the elementary counselor and is used with new staff, parenting groups, and community organizations.

2. *I Can Be at Home Alone* is a booklet developed to teach latchkey concepts. It is distributed and used in the third grade.

3. *Love Week, Rainbow Week, and We Are Family Week* are examples of districtwide guidance programs that are promoted throughout the schools and community.

4. *Traveling Troop* are dolls and curriculum that deal with understanding special needs students.

5. *Le Tres Chic* is a group guidance program that provides the opportunity for students to develop a positive self-concept through learning about hair and skin care, grooming, proper diet, and exercise.

6. *Peer Pressure Project* is a districtwide program for fifth grade that utilizes high school peer facilitators at the conclusion of a weeklong teacher taught project.

Evaluation

Counselors are requested to develop professional goals and objectives each year. These are reviewed and discussed with the program's supervisor periodically. These are both personal and districtwide in scope.

The guidance program is evaluated every 3 to 4 years by constructing a needs assessment instrument. The instrument is sent to parents, teachers, and administrators to receive input for change and improvement. A needs assessment is always conducted prior to program change.

Contact

James R. Jacobs
Assistant Director of Special Services
Eau Claire Area School District
500 Main Street
Eau Claire, Wisconsin 54701-3770
(715) 833-3471

Wynne Arkansas

Background

Wynne Intermediate School in Wynne, Arkansas, serves a community that is rural and primarily working class. The racial/ethnic background of the student body is 70% White and 30% Black.

The guidance program at the Wynne Intermediate School has existed for many years. It was identified as exemplary because, under the strong leadership of the counselor, it has continually expanded to develop new ideas and incorporate new lessons to meet the identified needs of both children and the broader society.

The primary focus is in the area of classroom guidance and small group counseling. In addition, its special strengths include programs on drug, alcohol, and tobacco education, personal safety, friendship skills, and helping children of divorce.

This guidance program serves children in grades 3, 4, and 5 at the intermediate school level. The counselor/student ratio is 1 to 470. Funding comes from the regular district budget.

Brief Program Description

The primary objectives of this intermediate school guidance and counseling program are to recognize the uniqueness of each student and to develop the mental, social, physical, and moral aspects of each child to enable each to function well in a changing society. The staff also strives to assist students to achieve their maximum potential. The basic counseling program is built around the areas of individual and small group counseling, consulting, and coordinating.

The major strength of this program is the supportive and cooperative staff and administration, and flexibility on the part of the community and the school to allow new ideas and programs to be implemented as new needs are identified. In addition to the strengths and exemplary features identified by the nominators of this program, several other highly effective practices are worthy of mention. One is the Student Host program, where students are chosen and trained to assist new students. Other examples of highly effective approaches to guidance are KATs (Kids are Terrific), a program of small group counseling for children of divorced parents, and the Friendship Program, which is designed to help students form good interpersonal relations and to make and keep friends.

It is interesting to note that this program was established 9 years ago with a counselor/student ratio of 1 to 1,350. The current ratio is considerably more manageable and allows for the development of activities that are a part of the school's regular curriculum.

Activities

The Student Host program is a group counseling program conducted over six sessions. The rationale is built around the fact that since 1970 almost half of all Americans aged 5 and over have changed their residence, often moving to a new school district. Such children need assistance in adjusting to their school and community.

The Student Host program has the following objectives:

1. New students will have friends on their first day at school, thereby easing the transition to a new school.
2. New students will have a reliable source of information from a Student Host.
3. The Student Host will develop skills to work effectively in a group setting and to improve social skills and acceptance of new and different people and to develop leadership skills.

PREPARING A STUDENT HOST

Session 1

- Get acquainted activities

- Explain duties/responsibilities of a Student Host

- Send notes home to parents

Session 2

- Group discussion of what it's like to be a new student

- Filmstrip "New Friends" (Learning Tree)

- Role play

Session 3

- Group discussion on meeting and greeting new students

- Learning and practicing role playing and making proper introductions

Session 4

- Presentation of Student Host badges

- Brainstorm list of important areas for new students
  Locations of offices and classrooms
  Rules for playground, cafeteria

- Provide written list for each student

Session 5

- Discuss additional responsibilities of a Student Host
  Collecting assignments for students who are absent
  Being a special friend to all new students

Session 6

- Presentation of certificates

- Group picture for local newspaper

- Refreshments

Teachers select student hosts twice yearly. Because a student may serve as a host only once, many students have the opportunity to be selected. This is not a program to choose the most popular students or the best academic students in each classroom. Often it identifies a student with low self-esteem to serve as a Student Host, thereby helping that student to gain confidence. A shy and withdrawn student may be the perfect choice for making friends with a new student. It may also be an excellent avenue for an "attention seeking" (alias behavior problem) student.

At the beginning of the six sessions of training, students receive a letter that indicates that they have been selected. It calls them to a planning meeting. A facsimile of the letter appears below. A certificate is presented at the end of the semester.

Dear _____

Congratulations! You have been chosen to serve as a Student Host for the spring semester of the 1988–89 school year. This is a big honor and responsibility for you. We are sure you will take the job seriously and do your very best.

Please meet with us and the others chosen to serve as a Student Host in your grade on this Friday at 1 pm in the counselor's office.

It is very important that you attend this meeting.

Respectfully,

Ms. Hull
Counselor

Evaluation

Evaluation of this guidance program is ongoing. It is often specific to the different activities the counselor presents. For example, the Student Host program is evaluated with a seven-item questionnaire for teachers who are asked to rate the effectiveness of the program as it relates to new students. Each Student Host is also asked to evaluate this program.

Contact

Sue Hull
Elementary Counselor
Wynne Intermediate School
P.O. Box 69
Wynne, AR 72396
(501) 238-2636

Orlando Florida

Background

Orange County Public Schools in Orlando, Florida, includes 73 elementary schools, each with an elementary school counselor. The Pinar Elementary School (grades K through 5) was nominated because its programs, which emphasize small group counseling, were considered exemplary.

The counselor/student ratio at Pinar is 1 to 725. The district serves a combination of urban, suburban, and rural settings. Representing a White middle-class community in general, the school also serves about 15% to 20% of students from a Hispanic background. Many are non-English speaking and receive instruction through an English as a Second Language program.

Special resources include programs for the learning disabled, programs for the gifted and talented, and a part-time speech and language class. The school receives the services of a psychologist and social worker on a part-time basis.

The present counselor has been assigned to this specific school for 10 years. She was the first elementary school counselor assigned to Pinar Elementary School, and consequently planned the initial counseling program.

Brief Program Description

The program at Pinar Elementary School was developed with input from a school guidance committee composed of volunteers who are professional staff members (mostly teachers). The philosophy of guidance at the school is drawn from that of Ashley Montagu, a noted anthropologist. His view that "by virtue of being born to humanity every human being has a right to the development and fulfillment of [his/her] potentialities as a human being" permeates all aspects of the program.

This developmental program has a heavy emphasis on counseling students in small groups. The major objectives of the program include:

• To counsel students both in groups and individually

• To consult with parents, administrators, teachers, and other professionals in school and community on behalf of students

• To coordinate referrals for special-needs students

• To develop classroom guidance activities to enhance self-awareness, positive habits and attitudes, understanding of human behavior, and decision-making skills

• To ensure that all students benefit from guidance

Activities

The counseling program at this school uses many excellent and varied activities and materials. One of the major strengths of the Pinar program is clear and detailed plans for initiating and facilitating new programs.

Emphasis for the 1988 school year was on nutrition and weight control groups and on divorce groups. Both were formed on a volunteer basis and were open to students in grades 3–5. Other small group counseling that has been offered in the Pinar program includes groups addressing self-concept, getting along with others, and improving behavior.

The counselor strongly believes that the use of small groups is the most effective form of counseling in an elementary school setting. This is especially true in an overcrowded elementary school curriculum.

A description of how three programs at Pinar operate appears below. The weight control program is described first, followed by the program on divorce. Lastly, the details of getting a new program on peer counseling off the ground are included.

The "Way-Less" program includes five major objectives:

- To acquaint students with a basic understanding of nutrition

- To help students understand the importance of proper exercise

- To assist students in making better food choices

- To build students' self-esteem

- To provide students with an awareness that will influence their eating behaviors in the future

The activities used in this program are outlined in the Guidelines, a portion of which is included.

GUIDELINES FOR RUNNING A WEIGHT CONTROL AND NUTRITION GROUP IN THE ELEMENTARY SCHOOL

• Counselor visits each classroom at appropriate grade levels to explain purpose of group: to study nutrition and ways to control weight. Number of meetings (6 to 8) and time and place are announced. Interested students are encouraged to enroll.

• Session 1—Each student is weighed initially and at each subsequent session. Actual weight is compared to appropriate weight range. Students are instructed in making charts to record food intake for the coming week. Students receive a letter to take to parents. Letter explains the program and advises parents to contact counselor if they have questions, concerns, or would like to attend the meetings.

• Sessions 2–3—Instruction in four basic food groups and the study of balanced diet habits and purpose of proteins, fats, carbohydrates, vitamins, and minerals for good nutrition. Discussion of family eating patterns and routines. Students encouraged to discuss the group with their parents at home.

• Sessions 4 to end—Discussions center on feelings about food, peer pressure, coping with unkind remarks. Discussion about continuing the good eating habits being established. Exercise, fitness, and "junk food" are discussed.

• Sessions augmented with filmstrips, tapes, and printed materials. Students encouraged to produce reports on various aspects of nutrition that can be presented and discussed in the group.

Guidelines for the divorce group also have been developed. The objectives are:

• To provide opportunities for students to share their feelings with others

• To help students understand that they are not alone

• To assist students in dealing with hostility and help them understand they are not to blame

• To give students some skills in coping with the situation

Some activities used in this program are included in the following Guidelines.

GUIDELINES FOR RUNNING A GROUP
FOR CHILDREN WHOSE PARENTS HAVE DIVORCED

• Counselor visits each classroom at appropriate grade levels to explain purpose of the group: an opportunity to discuss feelings about divorce and interact with others who are having similar problems. Participation in the group, which meets for 6 to 8 sessions, is voluntary and contingent upon parental permission.

  • Session 1—Counselor discusses group process, stresses importance of confidentiality. Balance of session is spent getting acquainted. Some students share feelings about divorce.

  • Sessions 2–5—Each session is opened with a filmstrip in the series *Coping With Your Parents' Divorce*, produced by Learning Tree. The filmstrips are designed to introduce topics for discussion. In Session 2, *A Broken Home* promotes discussion of assigning blame and introduces the concept that divorce might lead to happier lives. In Session 3, *Must You Choose Sides* explores feelings of children whose parents are engaging in custody disputes. Helps children understand that changes in behaviors of both parents and children are expected and appropriate.
  Session 4 uses *Full Time Parent/Weekend Parent* to stimulate discussion of how to adjust to not seeing one parent as often as in the past. Rejection by a parent and attendant hostility that is felt are discussed. *What if Mom/Dad Remarries?* is shown in session 5. It raises the issue of stepparents and leads to discussions of how children feel about remarriage. Helps group members understand that they can love a stepparent without minimizing love for a natural parent.

  • Session 6 to end. Group deals with ways to get individual help if needed. Resources for the counselor include *The Boys' and Girls' Book About Divorce* by Richard A. Gardner, MD. This is suitable both for children to read on their own or for use by a counselor with younger children. A second filmstrip series, *My Mother and Father are Getting Divorced* (Sunburst Communications), is sometimes used to supplement the other material.

Another example of careful and detailed planning is seen in an activity that is highly regarded at this school and by the counselor. It is the training of peer facilitators. Fifth-grade students receive 8 weeks of training in techniques of listening, problem solving, and giving feedback. They are then assigned as classroom helpers to teachers in kindergarten through grade 3.

Guidelines for this innovative use of peer facilitators also have been developed. The objectives of the peer group are:

- To provide trained, friendly helpers for primary teachers

- To help primary students by offering assistance in academics or opportunities for them to talk about their feelings

- To develop situations where peer helpers can develop their skills and enhance their self-esteem

- To assist peer helpers to understand and develop responsibility

- To enhance communication and interpersonal relationships between students at different age levels

The following information extracted from the Guidelines for Peer Facilitators illustrates some of the activities included in the peer facilitator program.

EXTRACTS FROM GUIDELINES FOR THE SELECTION AND TRAINING OF PEER FACILITATORS IN THE ELEMENTARY SCHOOL

• Counselor visits each fifth-grade classroom to explain the program and distribute applications. Appointments are made for individual interviews with counselor. At the interview the application is reviewed. Counselor and student discuss answers to the following questions on the application:

—Why do you want to be a peer facilitator?
—What jobs do you hold at home?
—What jobs have you held in the classroom?

Grades and classroom behavior are also considered. References are contacted. A contract that describes the responsibilities of a peer facilitator is signed by the student, parent, classroom teacher, and the counselor. Eight weekly training sessions begin after all students for the year have been selected.

• Sessions 1–2—Group discussions of friendship and the importance of helping others are held. Caring, understanding, accepting, and trusting are emphasized.

• Sessions 3–4—Focus on listening skills. *Children Helping Children*, developed by Myrick and Bowman, and *Magic Circle* techniques by Palomares and Ball are used as counselor resource materials.

• Sessions 5–6—Continue development of listening skills. Introduce open-ended questioning, clarifying, and summarizing statements and responding to feelings.

• Sessions 7–8—Continue the development of all skills introduced. Present problem-solving concepts and use of role playing to practice skills.

• After placement as peer facilitators, periodic meetings are held to discuss problems encountered and to update skills by further practice.

Evaluation

The elementary school counselor evaluates her program with input from a guidance committee composed of teachers. During monthly meetings, guidelines are set and input is provided to goals and objectives of the school guidance program. Over the years written needs assessments have been conducted. The results of these assessments, together with verbal feedback of teachers and other professional staff, have contributed to program development and evaluation.

Contact

Nancy Allen
Pinar School
3701 Anthony Lane
Orlando, FL 32822
(407) 277-6360

For information on the districtwide program contact:

Sara Timinski
Program Consultant in Elementary School Guidance
Orange County Public Schools
P.O. Box 271
Orlando, FL 32802
(407) 423-9244

La Porte
Indiana

Background

The Crichfield Elementary School is one of nine elementary schools in the La Porte, Indiana, Community Schools Corporation. The counselor/student ratio at this school is 1 to 750, and the districtwide student/counselor ratio is 1 to 625. This is an established program with funding from the regular school district budget. The community of La Porte is a combination of urban/rural, primarily of working class socioeconomic status, and is racially predominantly White.

Brief Program Description

This program has been implemented in the nine elementary schools (kindergarten through 5) and the two middle schools (6 through 8). The community prides itself on a program that is significantly different from other counseling programs in that counselors are not burdened with traditional activities such as testing or attending case conferences for special education. This allows the counselors to serve all children with developmental needs.

Unusual or highly effective practices in this program include a peer facilitator program, a child abuse unit introduced at grade 2, a transition program from kindergarten to grade one, and a study skills program at all grade levels. Crichfield Elementary School also features a developmental approach that has substantially reduced the need for crisis intervention counseling; topically oriented large group classroom guidance; and lunch groups, a social activity where children have lunch with the counselor.

Some of the large group classroom guidance units that have been developed serve up to 100 students. Counselor activity is divided between individual and small group counseling; large group classroom guidance and peer facilitation programs; consultation; and coordination of guidance services.

Activities

We have chosen to tell you a little about the large group classroom guidance activities the counselor at Crichfield Elementary School uses. These activities are different from what you might typically find. How the group is organized, how time is organized, and the specific structure of the activity are presented below, followed by a specific activity—"Wearing of Attitude Glasses"—used to illustrate how this activity works.

These large group classroom guidance activities or units have been developed in 30-minute time blocks. Each session is divided into four parts: an introduction (3–5 minutes), an initial activity (8–10 minutes), a second activity (8–10 minutes), and closure (5–10 minutes). The introduction is designed to gain the class's attention, prepare the students for the session, provide a transition from a previous session, and introduce the topic of the session. Activity one is counselor- or teacher-led with the total class. The second activity includes small group interaction with specific tasks. The closure is counselor- or teacher-led, again with the total class, and includes a summary of the session and assignment of out-of-class activities.

The counseling staff believes that time management is important. If additional time is available, further discussion is possible, but no guidance unit exceeds 45 minutes.

The guidance staff also believes that room arrangements are important. Students are shown how to participate in teams of approximately six students. The teams are positioned around the room in semicircles. During the initial activity the counselor speaks to the class via the semicircle groups. During the second activity the teams close their groups for discussion. They then reposition themselves in semicircles for the closure.

Such an organization reduces disruption, is a time saver, and maximizes the opportunity for student participation.

Each session has a topic, an idea, or a focus related to the purpose and goals of the guidance unit. Activities are structured procedures followed by opportunities to stimulate thinking and elicit discussion. The counselors and the teachers also model behaviors to help make the sessions a positive experience. Tests and inventories are frequently used to assess outcomes.

The following is an example of a session that uses this model of group guidance. It is entitled "Attitude Glasses." Its purpose is to help students recognize how attitudes affect their lives and how attitudes can be changed. Materials needed for this activity include glasses (imaginary or real frames) to dramatize this session, and a chalkboard or newsprint. This is session two in a six-session group guidance unit.

ATTITUDE GLASSES—SESSION TWO

INTRODUCTION: Begin by saying, "First, do you remember how we formed teams the last time we met? Let me see the hands of the first team. Do you remember where and how you sat for our class discussion? Okay. Now, let me see the hands of the second team (and so on)." Assign the teams to their positions in semicircles.

"Who remembers what we talked about last time? That's right, we talked about pleasant and unpleasant feelings. And, we also talked about how our feelings and the way we act are closely related. Let me see the hands of those who did the assignment—who took time to tell someone in the class about some feelings they noticed. What feelings did you notice?"

ACTIVITY I: Say, "Today I have some special glasses. They are called attitude glasses (write the word 'attitude' on the board). When you wear attitude glasses you also put on the same attitude as the glasses. In other words, you see things in that particular way."

Hold up a pair of glasses or pretend to take out a pair of glasses. "These attitude glasses are called Suspicious Glasses. What do you suppose a suspicious attitude is?" After a few responses put the glasses on and look over the class in a suspicious manner. Then say something like this: "Oh, just look at them sitting there. They're just waiting for me to make a mistake. They don't want to do things with me. They probably don't even want me to be here. I'll bet we don't have a very good discussion either. I wonder if they even like me? They probably say mean things about me after I leave, too!"

Have the teacher put on the same glasses and then tell him or her that the principal has asked for a meeting after school. The teacher might respond with, "I haven't done a thing wrong. I wonder what the problem is?"

Next, pull out another set of glasses and call these "Gloomy Glasses." Ask the class what gloomy means.

The session goes on in this vein, with a third pair of "Rosy Glasses" introduced. Examples are drawn from students. Students discuss other kinds of attitudes they might have and they are written on the board.

Activity two begins with the class discussing a situation that could be affected by attitudes. Each team is asked to pick one attitude they would like to act out in pantomime. Teams are also given the opportunity to talk about an attitude and to act it out.

Closure involves a discussion of such questions as: "What kind of world would it be if everyone wore the same kind of attitude?" or "Have there been days when you thought you had a particular set of attitude glasses on most of the day?"

A summary is provided with a statement that the way we go about work and play is often affected by our attitudes. Students are then given the assignment to wear their "Rosy Attitude Glasses" for the rest of the day.

Evaluation

The school district conducts research to determine the effectiveness of guidance units and subsequent changes in student learning behaviors. The school district is also interested in implementing a complete program to illustrate the concept of developmental counseling. Consequently Robert and Linda Myrick, university consultants, were employed for 5 years from the inception of the program to assist with training and evaluation of the program leading to its refinement at the present time.

Contact

Sara G. (Sally) Mayes
Elementary Guidance Counselor
La Porte Community School Corporation
Crichfield Elementary School
336 West Johnson Road
La Porte, IN 46350
(219) 362-2020

Amherst
Massachusetts

Background

Fort River Elementary School is one of four elementary schools in the Amherst, Massachusetts, Public School District. Each has at least one full-time guidance counselor. This is an established elementary school counseling program with funding from the regular district budget. Counselor/student ratio is 1 to 300, serving grades kindergarten through 6. The community is suburban and primarily middle class. Although this school community is predominantly White, 15% of the population is Black or Cambodian.

The program was nominated because of its focus on a consultant model, in which the counselor works with parents, teachers, and children. The counselor has identified levels of developmental assessment and counseling strategies that are used extensively in carrying out this program.

Brief Program Description

The counselor at Fort River Elementary School has identified 11 specific functions and activities.

1. *Individual and group counseling.* Approximately 30% of the student population is seen in a given year. Sessions range from a brief number of one-to-one encounters to counseling on a regular basis for a semester or more. The goal of group counseling is to teach children to listen to one another and to work through problems in interpersonal areas before they become serious concerns.

2. *Consultation with teachers.* The counselor at Fort River holds weekly meetings with each teacher. The focus is behavioral management, social/emotional concerns of children, and strategies to improve academic performance.

3. *Parent meetings.* The counselor averages 10 to 12 parent conferences weekly. The complexity ranges from discussion of how to work with a gifted child to referral for more complex problems.

4. *Classroom visits.* The counselor conducts five to six classroom visits each week to observe children, follow up on behavioral management, conduct a group, or just for informal contact with teacher and children.

5. *Special education.* The counselor is the first school staff member after the teacher to be involved in referral to special education. She consults with the teacher in order to make the best educational placement for each child. The counselor conducts home visits and continues counseling special education students when recommended by the special education team.

6. *Inservice.* The counselor conducts workshops for classroom teachers and others on such topics as environmental influences on student behavior, divorce, developing student self-esteem, and career education. Some of these programs are supported through grants written by the counselor.

7. *Testing.* Diagnostic testing around issues of intellectual functioning and reading is provided for several children each year. Kindergarten and first-grade screening at the beginning of the school year is also a part of the counselor's responsibilities to the district testing program.

8. *Orientation and transition*. The counselor conducts an interview with each new student. Many parents also are interviewed at this time. A transition program from kindergarten to first grade is currently under development. Transition programs for sixth graders moving to the junior high school is conducted each spring.

9. *Committee work*. The counselor holds membership on a number of school district committees, including the inservice team planning committee that is responsible for coordinating the training and support services for all inservice teams that serve the Amherst Area Teaching Center.

10. *Special programs*. This activity varies according to the needs of the school community. Recent examples of special programs include a career education unit, drug education, sex education, and communication skills. The counselor also conducts an evening parent education course once or more yearly.

11. *Crisis intervention*. The counselor is usually the first school official to come into contact with crisis situations. These may range from the child who is reacting to a crisis situation at home and disrupts the classroom, to self-referred children whose crises are very real to them, or to parents who are unable to cope with their children. The counselor task here is to assess the situation and assist in developing a plan of action. Frequently this includes referral to another agency.

Activities

Of great interest are the four levels of developmental assessment and counseling strategies that are utilized in this program. The levels of sensorimotor, concrete operations, formal operations, and dialectic/systems have been developed by the counselor, Mary Bradford Ivey, and Allen E. Ivey, of the University of Massachusetts.

Children at the elementary school primarily operate at the sensorimotor and concrete leves. Specific questioning strategies tend to be more effective if they are matched to the child's developmental level. Mary and Allen Ivey have found that most children with a skilled counselor can learn a type of more complex formal operational thinking. The following material can be used as a practice exercise that brings developmental concepts into the elementary guidance interview. Most effective counselors already use these techniques—the developmental model here simply points out their relationship to Piagetian constructs and provides some beginning ideas for facilitating cognitive growth.

The ideas here were derived from Allen Ivey's book, *Developmental Therapy* (San Franciso: Jossey-Bass, 1986) and an article by Mary and Allen Ivey that has been submitted for publication. The authors would be glad to share additional material with those who are interested. The authors give permission for xeroxing of the following material if credit for authorship and the address of Mary Ivey is included on the handouts.

Developmental assessment and counseling strategies associated with each level are briefly described below, together with some suggestions to facilitate movement over the four cognitive developmental levels.

Clients may be expected to present their problems and issues from four levels of meaning-making. Younger children will generally discuss their problems at a sensorimotor, or concrete level. Some fifth and sixth graders may be expected to present themselves with formal operational issues. Relatively few individuals (children or adults) will present their issues at the postformal, dialectic/systemic level.

Once the counselor assesses the child's cognitive-developmental level, then it is possible to institute developmentally appropriate interventions.

Sensorimotor (What are the *elements* of experience?)

Assessment: The child presents problems in a random fashion, jumps topics frequently, and may show examples of magical or irrational thinking. Behavior will tend to follow the same pattern in terms of short attention span and frequent body movement.

Treatment: An environmental structuring approach is useful, in which the counselor provides a firm foundation for exploring randomness, later providing the structure for growth. In terms of interviewing techniques, listening skills, closed questioning to provide structuring, frequent paraphrasing, and summarization are useful. Direction is provided when needed. Examples of treatments may involve play therapy and games, body movement exercises, behavioral educational plans, and direct instruction in social skills.

Concrete Operations (Searching for *situational* descriptions)

Assessment: Most elementary children represent this mode of meaning making. They may talk endlessly with small details of their experience. Their difficulty, of course, is making a larger gestalt of their issues. Behaviorally, at issue is action and the developing awareness of "if..., then..." causal thinking.

Treatment: The counselor acts more as a coach, alternating between direct action and structuring and careful listening. The child needs help in further organizing thought and behavioral patterns. Behavioral techniques and reality therapy are particularly helpful. When dealing with cognitive problems of causal thinking, Adlerian logical consequences methods or adaptations of Ellis's frames may be helpful.

Formal Operations (What *patterns* of thought may be discerned?)

Assessment: The child who is searching to make meaning of the self is a prime example of formal operational issues. Here the individual is trying to see patterns of the self and we find the "self looking to find self." In described self or situations, we may ask "Is that a pattern?" or "Does that happen in other situations?" If the child can see the underlying structural repetitions, he or she is showing signs of formal thinking.

Treatment: The elementary counselor often has difficulty here because the treatment requires the counselor to operate more as a consultant and to place more power in the meaning-making capability of the child. This requires a shift in the counselor's methods and perceptions and placing more control in the hands of the child. Formal operational theories of the self and the pattern mode of thinking abound and include Rogerian, cognitive-behavior, psychodynamic, and many others.

Dialectic/Systemic (How did that develop in a *system* or how is all this *integrated*?)

Assessment: Most children and adults do not ordinarily make sense of their worlds from this frame of reference. In children, dialectic/systemic thinking will manifest itself most clearly when young women (usually in the upper grades) start talking seriously about sexism, or when minority students recognize that their difficulties may be caused by a racist system. Here the child is operating on systems of knowledge and is learning how he or she is affected by the environment. The locus of control changes from the individual child or teacher to larger systemic concerns. As counselors, we should be aware that family and classrooms are two important systems affecting the child that need more consideration and analysis.

Treatment: Systems thinking is manifested in family therapy and in class-room consultation. We also use systems orientations when we help children deal individually or in groups with issues of racism, sexism, and handicapping conditions. When we go to a case conference with our colleagues and the family, we are utilizing our dialectic/systemic skills. In terms of individual work, when we ask children how they integrate their sensorimotor, concrete, and formal experiences, we are moving toward the dialectic/systemic frame of reference.

In the following section, examples of developmental therapy systemic questioning are presented.

FACILITATING MOVEMENT OVER THE FOUR COGNITIVE-DEVELOPMENTAL LEVELS © 1988

Opening developmental therapy questions:

"Could you tell me what's bothering you?" "What's up?" or some alternative opening.
Your goal: 50 or more words so you can assess developmental functioning.
Is the child or adult client presenting as:

- S-M random, emotions
- Concrete linear description
- Formal self-examination and analytical
- Dialectic/systemic awareness of how self is affected by the system

Join the child or client where he or she is developmentally. Summarize the opening.

Sensorimotor:

Your goal: Elaboration of the issue as it is presented by the child. Permit introduction of random elements.
Sample questions: Imagine the person or situation—get a specific image in your mind. What do you SEE? HEAR? FEEL?
Paraphrase, reflect feelings, and summarize periodically to facilitate coordination and organization of data.

Concrete operations:

Your goal: Clear linear description of events.
Sample questions: Could you give a specific example? What did he say? What did she do? What happened before? After? If you do that, then what happens?
Paraphrase, reflect feelings, and summarize periodically to facilitate coordination and organization of data.

Formal Operations or pattern:

Your goal: To bring out repeating patterns of situations or self-examination.
Sample questions: Does that happen in other situations? Is that a pattern? Does it happen a lot? Have you felt like that in other places?
Paraphrase, reflect feelings, and summarize periodically to facilitate coordination and organization of data.

Dialectic/systemic:

Your goal: To see how the child puts it together OR to encourage systems and family thinking.
Sample questions: How do you put together what we have talked about? What one thing stands out for you? How does this work in your family? What rule is your family operating under? What are you going to do about it? What's the flaw in that rule?
Paraphrase, reflect feelings, and summarize periodically to facilitate coordination and organization of data.

Evaluation

Each elementary school counselor develops a written annual plan as part of this school district's management-by-objectives scheme of evaluation. The components of the plan include goals, operational strategies, and activities associated with each goal. Discussions about the plan's components are held between the counselor and the building principal at the start of the school year and reviewed each spring to ensure that the program goals are being achieved.

Contact

Mary Bradford Ivey
Elementary Counselor
Fort River Elementary School
70 South East Street
Amherst, MA 01002
(413) 253-9731

Rochester
Minnesota

Background

Independent School District (ISD) Number 535, located in Rochester, Minnesota, enrolls 7,200 elementary students in 16 schools. The Jefferson Elementary Guidance Program is a unique program in this school district. One counselor serves the 730 students at Jefferson.

The community is urban, primarily upper-middle class, and predominantly White. Special resources include a guidance committee composed of teachers, students, parents, and the counselor. Initially funded by Northwest Area Foundation grant money, within a few years after its inception this program became a regular part of the Jefferson Elementary School's budget.

Brief Program Description

The counseling program at this school began from scratch in 1984. It came about as a result of a project to identify ideas related to self-directed learning through school-based management. Eleven committees were formed, one of which was a guidance committee. Its purpose was to develop a program that would meet individual needs of students and enhance their social and emotional development as self-directed learners. The personnel committee interviewed and hired the counselor to implement the program.

The guidance committee had developed a plan for an instructional program that would emphasize the social and emotional growth of each student. A thorough understanding of the developmental levels of childhood was needed by the Jefferson community. This understanding is especially important in this program because of the philosophy on which the program is based, that of the self-directed learner.

The guidance program emphasizes affective educational programming for children and a strong parent education component. It includes crisis intervention and short-term counseling.

Major strengths of this program are its numerous classroom guidance activities. A unit approach is used, and the counselor meets with each class in three 5-week cycles per year. Teachers include a commercially developed affective curriculum, "Positive Action," 4 days per week, with the counselor serving as a resource to the teacher. The counselor also offers a parent education program built around commercial materials entitled "Active Parenting."

Activities

Because this program was new and involved only one counselor, emphasis was placed on locating existing materials that would enhance the guidance program objectives. Rather than developing entirely new materials, it was decided that current resources would be identified and either used as they were or adapted to the special needs of the Jefferson Elementary Guidance Program.

Recent materials were identified in such areas as program planning, program evaluation, curriculum scope and sequence, and developmental guidance. A resource list was developed by the Jefferson Elementary School counselor. Examples of the kinds of materials included are given below.

EXAMPLES FROM A RESOURCE LIST

Program planning (includes this recent book and four journal articles taken from *The School Counselor*)

> Myrick, R. D. (1987). *Developmental guidance and counseling: A practical approach.* Minneapolis: Educational Media Corporation.

Program evaluation (includes three journal articles, one of which provides an example of guidance program evaluation)

> Lewis, J. (1983). Guidance program evaluation: How to do it. *The School Counselor, 31*, 111–119.

Curriculum scope and sequence materials (includes materials developed by four different state or local school districts) including:

> North Carolina Department of Public Instruction. (1985). *Teacher handbook: Guidance K–12 subject by subject. North Carolina competency based curriculum.* Raleigh, NC: Author.

> Racine Unified School District. (1984). *SGS student guidance system grades K–12. Developmental guidance and counseling.* Racine, WI: Author.

> Iowa Department of Education. (1986). *Iowa K–12 career guidance curriculum guide for student development.* Des Moines, IA: Author.

> Wisconsin Department of Public Instruction. (1986). *School counseling programs: A resource and planning guide.* Madison, WI: Author.

Developmental guidance curriculum materials with classroom activities (includes six different resources drawn from North Carolina, Florida, South Dakota, and Wisconsin) including:

Lake County, Florida, Public Schools. (1985). *Schoolwide experiences in affective learning. SEAL patrol.* Tavarres, FL: Author.

Guilford County School System. (1985). *The school guidance and counseling resource manual K–5.* Greensboro, NC: Author.

Menasha Joint School District. (1983). *Menasha developmental guidance curriculum.* Menasha, WI: Author.

Osseo-Fairchild School District. (1984). *Osseo-Fairchild developmental guidance curriculum.* Osseo, WI: Author.

Sioux Falls School District 49–5. (date unavailable). *Developmental guidance and counseling plan for kindergarten through sixth grade.* Sioux Falls, SD: Author.

Winneconne Community School District. (1988). *Winneconne developmental guidance curriculum.* Winneconne, WI: Author.

Commercially prepared kits (such as the DUSO-R or Project Charlie) for counselor classroom work, materials for teachers, and materials for counselors to use with groups are included as well.

This list moves beyond the traditional types of areas and draws from topics that reflect current concerns in the broader society. In so doing it identifies current journal articles on topics such as moving and relocation, crisis and death, divorce, and latchkey children. The reader may wish to contact the school district for a complete list of the resources currently used.

Evaluation

This elementary school guidance program was evaluated through the efforts of a guidance committee at the end of year 1 and year 2 of operation. The committee conducted a survey of the staff of the Jefferson Elementary School, the parents, and the students by using a questionnaire. Results indicated strong support from all three groups. The counselor was able to develop a high level of trust in 1 year. Results of the evaluation were used to develop guidance objectives for the following year. Currently, an evaluation and needs assessment is scheduled every 3 years.

Contact

Jane Bogan
Elementary Counselor
Jefferson Elementary School
1201 10th Avenue, N.E.
Rochester, MN 55904
(507) 281-6091

Columbia
South Carolina

Background

The Studio G developmental guidance program at Forest Lake Elementary School in the Richland School District Two in Columbia, South Carolina, is an example of a fully developed program of individual and small group counseling, classroom guidance, consultation, and coordination that was established in less than 2 years. Studio G operates in one school with an enrollment of approximately 600 students, grades kindergarten through 5, plus special education classes. The community is suburban, primarily middle class, and predominantly White. Primary financial support for the program comes from the regular district budget.

The hallmark of the program is that it reflects a team effort of a counselor, administrators, teachers, aides, and students working together to design and implement a successful guidance and counseling program. The program has been featured in newspaper and magazine articles throughout South Carolina.

Brief Program Description

A major strength of the program is the developmental classroom guidance emphasis. All students in the 26 classes at Forest Lake Elementary School receive formal lessons on a regularly scheduled basis. Other notable elements include the group guidance program, which served more than 400 students in the first year of operation.

Other features of this guidance program include a structured parent education program, and a special newsletter published monthly to promote effective community education. Community resources are used extensively in this guidance program.

One highly effective approach in the Forest Lake Elementary School program is the G Force, a fourth- and fifth-grade peer facilitator program. Additional funds were obtained to develop a Guidance Material Resource Center that has a wide array of multimedia materials on more than 60 guidance topics. The counselor also finds time to serve as a field supervisor for university students preparing to be school counselors who are assigned on an intern and practicum basis.

Activities

The counselor at Forest Lake is very involved in classroom guidance activities. Within his highly structured schedule, he plans regular meetings with each of the six grades to work on a common theme. For example, at the beginning of the school year he plans a unit called "Getting Ready." He sets two objectives for each student: (1) each student will define personal goals and ways to attain them, and (2) each student will identify at least one personal goal for the school year. Follow-up activities involve having students and teachers chart individual and classroom goals that are developed for the year.

Interested in ensuring that all students and faculty know about his comprehensive guidance program, this counselor has developed a one-page announcement describing the areas of emphasis for his program. An example of the type of announcement used describes seven areas for the guidance program.

AREAS OF EMPHASIS IN OUR COUNSELING PROGRAM

Counseling: Individual and small group sessions are available to help our children understand and cope with their concerns.

New Students: The guidance counselor can assist you in helping our new students to adjust positively to a new school setting by providing "Welcome to Forest Lake" sessions for the students.

Consulting: The door is always open for educators and parents to come in for the purpose of discussing the needs of our children.

Discussion Groups: The guidance counselor is available to organize and conduct parenting programs as well as special interest discussion groups for parents or educators.

Resource Center: Our counselor can help you plan lessons or units of study. Materials are available on over 60 topics.

Classroom Lessons: Every homeroom in the school will be visited on a regular, consistent, and scheduled basis. Students will receive developmental and preventive lessons covering a wide variety of guidance-related topics.

Special Lessons: Teachers can always request additional classroom lessons to address specific classroom needs or to assist with grade-level units of study.

Such announcements make it clear to teachers that this counselor is available to help them and their students. He is not sitting in his office waiting for something to happen. Rather he is actively involved in developmental activities that address the needs of all students.

Evaluation

The Studio G program was designed based upon an annual needs assessment in which parents, staff members, and students participated. It is evaluated on a 9-week basis by the counselor, who reports activities conducted in each of the major elements of the program. Subsequent needs assessments help to determine future directions of the program.

Contact

Ron Miles
School Counselor
Forest Lake Elementary School
6801 Brookfield Road
Columbia, SC 29206
(803) 782-0470

SECTION THREE

MORE NEW IDEAS

A questionnaire was designed to obtain information about the special features and innovative practices of the programs nominated for recognition as exemplary guidance and counseling programs. In the preceding section we have highlighted 10 of those programs, those chosen as exemplary by our blue ribbon committee. We wanted to include in this book in a summary fashion information reported about all programs whose representatives responded to our request for information. Therefore, data reported by the 134 respondents were reviewed and summarized with an eye to providing elementary school counselors information about current programs and practices.

In order to describe these programs more meaningfully, the information taken from the questionnaire was categorized and summarized into several domains that represent the major emphases of elementary counseling and guidance. These domains include **classroom guidance, small group counseling, individual counseling, consultation,** and **coordination**. Subareas within each domain were also included. We developed a matrix using these domains as headings, and added a column to indicate unique components.

This matrix of all programs, alphabetized by state, is reproduced at the end of this section. We think it is an extremely valuable summary of information in that it enables you to identify at a glance both how programs are alike and in what ways they are unusual. It should reinforce you in your efforts to build a new program or improve an existing one. By comparing your own program with others around the country, you can begin to see how yours is similar to others and how it is different.

What can we say about these programs by looking at this matrix? One of our first observations is that the vast majority of the programs are developmental and preventive in nature. Consequently these programs are most often available to all students, not only those who are experiencing difficulty. One of the unfortunate misconceptions about elementary counseling and guidance often held by those not directly associated with the field is that an elementary school counselor's primary function is to serve students who are in a crisis or are in need of special services. Parents and other educators often have difficulty understanding the role of the counselor as a developmental specialist. School personnel across the country in districts that are starting elementary counseling programs are constantly being asked: What is the role of the counselor? What is he or she supposed to do? How are counselors different from school psychologists or social workers? These representative programs attest to the fact that the elementary counselor is there to serve all children, not only those in trouble.

A second observation gleaned from the matrix is that most programs are designed to promote student development in the areas of sound and realistic self-concept, interpersonal skills, decision making, and academic development. Notice that at the elementary school level the areas of personal and social development are emphasized as frequently as is academic development. This counseling function differs somewhat from the emphasis at the secondary level, where the counselor is often seen as being there to assist with future plans, whether they be postsecondary education or direct entry into the labor market.

Another observation is that the counselor doesn't see his or her role as working independently of teachers and parents. Most programs stress the active involvement of parents through volunteer activities and parent groups. Many include teachers as an integral part of the programs, especially in those localities where the counselor/student ratio is high. In such areas, teachers often conduct classroom guidance activities in consultation with the counselor.

Finally, a large number of programs emphasize the importance of regular program evaluation to determine program effectiveness and to make necessary improvements. The inclusion of evaluation is key to recognizing that guidance is an integral part of the total school curriculum. If the results of guidance efforts are not seen, then guidance will remain only tangential to the total school program.

In addition to describing the common elements of these 134 elementary guidance and counseling programs, we have identified what we considered to be unique components or features of some of the programs. We've picked some to tell you about in detail.

Many of these unique program elements relate to developmental guidance activities. The "Success Express" operating in Memphis, Tennessee, is an elementary dropout prevention program. It begins before first grade to address dropout prevention through early intervention strategies for high-risk students. The program emphasizes the developmental guidance components of self-concept and self-awareness, values clarification and decision-making skills, social and communication skills, career and educational goals, and stress and time management.

Some of the unique programs illustrate the great interest in the role counselors play in dealing with personal and social issues children at the elementary level face. Bentonville, Arkansas, has a program called "Miss Pickle." This program is used as an introductory and self-referral system with first and second graders. Children are taught the saying that "Life is like a pickle. Sometimes it's sweet, sometimes it's sour, and sometimes it's in-between." A counselor is described as someone you can talk to when your life is sweet, sour, or in-between. Children who want to talk to the counselor write their name and room number on a piece of paper and put it in Miss Pickle's mailbox, located outside the counselor's office.

"Talking Turns" is a program that comes out of Long Beach, California. The major strength of talking turns is the requirement that students refer themselves for small group guidance. The discussions relate to issues that are important to children. Students develop problem-solving skills. They gain insight into counseling as a healthy and normal activity. They develop insight into themselves and others through reflective listening and honest disclosure.

In Las Vegas, Nevada, teachers and other staff members use "Gotcha" tokens, badges, or stickers to reinforce positive and appropriate behaviors of students.

Some of the activities center around counselors working with teachers and other staff members. Dodge City, Kansas, has the "Hug Jug." The program is described in this way: All staff members are given hug jug coupons throughout the year. Staff members fill out coupons to recognize thoughtful gestures by co-workers, and place them in the hug jug in the office. Every 2 weeks at faculty meetings, a name is drawn from the hug jug, and that person chooses a gift from the gift table. The gift table includes teacher-donated craft items, business-donated products or services, parent-donated aide time, and baked goods, to name just a few. The teacher or staff member receives the hug award, and the rest of the hug coupons are placed in the individual teacher mailboxes to be read by the staff members who were recognized. Several teachers have started using the hug jug and coupons in their individual classrooms.

A Teacher Survival Kit has been developed by the counselor in Irmo, South Carolina. This involves a ziploc bag with fun items and a welcome sheet that is placed in each teacher's mailbox on the first day of school. A coupon book made up by the counselor may also be given to these new teachers, who can exchange them at a later date for ideas.

In Norfolk, Virginia, "GRIN" (Guidance Really Is Neat) folders are designed to assist teachers with classroom guidance. A folder is provided to each teacher at the beginning of the year, and activities are added periodically by the counselor.

The PALS (Positive Affective Learning Situations) program operating in Atglen, Pennsylvania, involves a group of teachers who, with leadership from the counselor, volunteer their time to provide positive experiences for the school. Examples of such activities include warm fuzzy week, make-a-friend month, truck day, and noncompetitive activities for field day.

Other unique programs or practices address special needs children might have. Hartford City, Indiana, runs a program called "Shampoo Parties." In this program children come to school early each Friday. They have breakfast, wash their hair, and talk about cleanliness. These are children who come from homes where there is no hot water and where there is extreme poverty.

Sheboygan, Wisconsin, runs a "Banana Split" group that is designed for children whose families have split up or whose home life involves dramatic change.

The "Choosy Chewers" program in St. Joseph, Missouri, is a diet and fitness club for overweight students.

Now it is up to you to look at other ways you can use the matrix. Beginning counselors might want to compare their new program with other programs in the state. They might want to see if the types of activities they are offering are similar to those offered by other programs. Counselors could go first to the entries under their state, and then look at the specific areas included for a particular domain. An experienced counselor anxious to expand the emphasis in a program from classroom guidance to include individual counseling might use the entries under the domain "individual" to demonstrate to their principals that many activities are included in a total guidance program and widely used throughout the country.

Other information provided in the matrix includes the student/counselor ratio for each program and the type of setting in which the program is located (e.g., urban, suburban, or rural). We are certain that you will think of other ways to use the matrix to improve your guidance and counseling program. Most of all we hope you will contact the leaders of these programs and others nominated to exchange ideas of mutual interest.

The 134 elementary guidance programs described in the matrix include programs from 40 states plus the District of Columbia and Puerto Rico. This represents all of the programs nominated as exemplary whose representatives responded to our request to complete the questionnaire describing their efforts. Almost all respondents included sample materials in support of their nomination. Our analysis of the questionnaires and supporting materials formed the basis of the matrix. We want to suggest that you contact the person indicated in the list of programs that you will find in the appendix to confirm what we report and to obtain other information about these exemplary programs. We also want to point out that the list includes all 183 programs that were nominated together with a contact person and an address. Representatives of some of these programs chose not to participate in the project and did not complete the questionnaires. In several cases the information that was sent was not usable. Nevertheless we wanted to include the basic identifying data about every program that was nominated.

We wish to thank several graduate students at Virginia Tech who were studying to be counselors for their role in developing the matrix. They include Ann Ferrell and Patti Talbot of the Montgomery County, Virginia School Division; Beverly Haun of Pulaski County, Virginia Schools; and Charlotte Williamson of Craig County, Virginia Public Schools.

MATRIX OF EXEMPLARY ELEMENTARY SCHOOL GUIDANCE AND COUNSELING PROGRAMS

Program Location	St:Co Ratio	Classroom Guidance											Small Group							Individual			Consultant				Coordination				Unique Component(s)
		Self-Concept	Self-Awareness	Study Skills	Decision Making	Communication	Interpersonal	Coping-Stress	Career	Testing	Substance Abuse	Personal Safety/Health	Peer Tutoring/Counseling	Student Development	Student Host	Special Needs	Motivation/School Attitudes	Attendance/"At Risk"	Interpersonal	Testing/Screening	Crisis Counseling	Special Needs	Parent	Teacher	Administration	Specialists	In-System Referral	Out-of-System Resources	School Testing/Screening	Evaluation of Program	
Alabama																															
1. Auburn (U)	490:1			×	×				×															×							Saturday/After School Study
2. Birmingham (U)	850:1										×												×	×	×						
3. Huntsville (U/S)	500:1	×		×			×				×				×	×					×	×	×	×		×	×	×			
4. Russell Co. (R)	514:1							×																							
5. Tuscaloosa (U)	610:1	×														×							×	×		×	×	×			"At Home Alone"

80

Location	Ratio	Program
Arkansas		
6. Bentonville (R)	450:1	"Miss Pickle" Self-Referral Program
7. Conway (S)	400:1	
8. Newark (R)	280:1	Mother/Daughter Preadolescent Preparation Program
9. Springdale (R)	600:1	Early Prevention of School Failure
10. Wynne (R)	470:1	
California		
11. Ceres (R/U)	600:1	
12. Long Beach (U)	1,125:1	"Talking Turns" Self-Referral Program, New Counselor Orientation Breakfast
13. San Diego (U)	1,700:1	
14. Stockton (S)	880:1	
Colorado		
15. Ft. Collins (R/S)	580:1	Intensive Kindergarten Program
16. Gilcrest*	220:1	"Being Me Is Special"
17. Kersey (R)	475:1	"Connections"
18. Platteville*	600:1	"Being Me Is Special"
Connecticut		
19. Bethel (R)	575:1	
District of Columbia		
20. (Washington DC) (U)	300:1	Peer Counseling

U = Urban   S = Suburban   R = Rural   * = Unreported

MATRIX OF EXEMPLARY ELEMENTARY SCHOOL GUIDANCE AND COUNSELING PROGRAMS

Program Location	St:Co Ratio	Classroom Guidance											Small Group							Individual			Consultant				Coordination				Unique Component(s)
		Self-Concept	Self-Awareness	Study Skills	Decision Making	Communication	Interpersonal	Coping-Stress	Career	Testing	Substance Abuse	Personal Safety/Health	Peer Tutoring/Counseling	Student Development	Student Host	Special Needs	Motivation/School Attitudes	Attendance/"At Risk"	Interpersonal	Testing/Screening	Crisis Counseling	Special Needs	Parent	Teacher	Administration	Specialists	In-System Referral	Out-of-System Resources	School Testing/Screening	Evaluation of Program	
Delaware																															
21. Milford (S)	820:1	×						×			×												×	×	×	×				×	
22. New Castle (S)	500:1	×					×				×					×	×									×					Use of Guitar, Puppetry Program
Florida																															
23. Gainesville [a] (S)	537:1					×			×		×		×				×						×	×	×	×	×	×			Minority Parent Program, Outreach Program on Child Abuse
24. Gainesville [b] (U)	450:1	×		×	×	×	×		×		×		×			×							×	×	×	×	×	×		×	"The Career Club", Minority Achievement Project

Location	Ratio	Unique Counseling Intervention for Exceptional Education Students	Weight Watchers Club	Creative Work in Developmental Play	"Pumsy"—Self-Esteem Enhancement	Relaxation Groups	"Stress Busters" Dropout Prevention	Parents Hour at School	Career Awareness Program (8th Grade)
25. Gainesville [c] (U/S)	582:1	x							
26. Newberry (R)	430:1	x							
27. Orlando [a] (S)	400:1	x							
28. Orlando [b] (S)	572:1								
29. Orlando [c] (S)	650:1	x	x						
30. Tampa [a] (U)	650:1								
31. Tampa [b] (S)	950:1			x					
Georgia									
32. Brunswick (S)	650:1	x							
33. Buford (R)	750:1	x							
34. Cumming [a] (R/S)	1,400:1				x				
35. Cumming [b] (R/S)	1,600:1					x			
36. Dalton (S)	750:1						x		
37. Douglasville (S)	500:1	x						x	
38. Lawrenceville (U/R/S)	900:1	x							
39. Savannah (U)	600:1	x							
Illinois									
40. Havana (R)	350:1								x

U = Urban   S = Suburban   R = Rural   * = Unreported

83

MATRIX OF EXEMPLARY ELEMENTARY SCHOOL GUIDANCE AND COUNSELING PROGRAMS

Program Location	St:Co Ratio	Classroom Guidance											Small Group							Individual			Consultant				Coordination				Unique Component(s)
		Self-Concept	Self-Awareness	Study Skills	Decision Making	Communication	Interpersonal	Coping-Stress	Career	Testing	Substance Abuse	Personal Safety/Health	Peer Tutoring/Counseling	Student Development	Student Host	Special Needs	Motivation/School Attitudes	Attendance/"At Risk"	Interpersonal	Testing/Screening	Crisis Counseling	Special Needs	Parent	Teacher	Administration	Specialists	In-System Referral	Out-of-System Resources	School Testing/Screening	Evaluation of Program	
Indiana																															
41. Hartford City (R)	700:1	x	x				x					x		x		x	x	x	x				x	x		x		x			Shampoo Parties, BUG Awards, CUBS Honors Breakfast
42. Hoagland (S/R)	650:1	x	x	x	x	x	x	x	x					x				x					x	x	x	x					
43. La Porte (U/R)	750:1	x	x	x	x	x	x	x	x	x		x	x	x	x			x				x		x	x						
44. Richmond (U)	1,171:1										x	x	x									x	x	x	x	x	x				Parent Workshops
45. Terre Haute (U/S/R)	950:1	x	x		x							x			x								x	x		x			x		
Iowa																															
46. Des Moines (S)	650:1							x			x			x		x						x	x	x							Boys Town Model on Social Skills

84

Kansas

	Ratio	Notes
47. Burlington (R)	340:1	
48. Dodge City (S/R)	715:1	"Hug Jug" for Staff
49. Olathe (S)	400:1	

Kentucky

	Ratio	Notes
50. Louisville (S/R)	325:1	"Reading, Set, Go" (Readiness for School) "Project Amigo"

Louisiana

	Ratio	Notes
51. Baton Rouge (U/R/S)	440:1	Lending Library for Parents
52. Lafayette (U)	800:1	
53. New Orleans [a] (U)	400:1	
54. New Orleans [b] (U)	170:1	
55. New Orleans [c] (U)	189:1	
56. Shreveport (S)	234:1	Test Buster Pep Rally

Maine

	Ratio	Notes
57. Auburn (U)	575:1	
58. Bucksport (R)	600:1	

Maryland

	Ratio	Notes
59. Annapolis*	950:1	

U = Urban   S = Suburban   R = Rural   * = Unreported

MATRIX OF EXEMPLARY ELEMENTARY SCHOOL GUIDANCE AND COUNSELING PROGRAMS

Program Location	St:Co Ratio	Classroom Guidance											Small Group							Individual			Consultant				Coordination				Unique Component(s)
		Self-Concept	Self-Awareness	Study Skills	Decision Making	Communication	Interpersonal	Coping-Stress	Career	Testing	Substance Abuse	Personal Safety/Health	Peer Tutoring/Counseling	Student Development	Student Host	Special Needs	Motivation/School Attitudes	Attendance/"At Risk"	Interpersonal	Testing/Screening	Crisis Counseling	Special Needs	Parent	Teacher	Administration	Specialists	In-System Referral	Out-of-System Resources	School Testing/Screening	Evaluation of Program	
Massachusetts																															
60. Amherst (S)	300:1								×		×			×		×							×	×				×			
61. Charlemont (R)	200:1								×															×							After School Family Counseling
Minnesota																															
62. New Ulm (R)	1,300:1							×	×				×			×					×	×	×	×	×	×	×	×			
63. Northfield (R)	1,375:1																									×					
64. Pine Island (R)	600:1															×					×		×	×			×			×	
65. Rochester (U)	730:1	×	×												×	×					×		×	×			×				

Location	Pupil Ratio	Program Notes
Mississippi		
66. Walls (R)	700:1	
Missouri		
67. St. Joseph*	1,000+:1	"Choosy Chewsers" Diet/Fitness Club
Nebraska		
68. Kearney (R)	800:1	Big Friend Program (for Students in Need)
69. Ogallala (R)	515:1	Screened H.S. Students Help Elementary
70. Omaha*	1,206:1	
Nevada		
71. Las Vegas (U)	1,200:1	"Gotcha"—Behavior Incentive
New York		
72. Clifton Park (S)	45:1	
73. Newburgh (S)	549:1	
74. Sidney (R)	700:1	
75. Walton (R)	840:1	
New Mexico		
76. Las Vegas (R)	*	

U = Urban S = Suburban R = Rural * = Unreported

MATRIX OF EXEMPLARY ELEMENTARY SCHOOL GUIDANCE AND COUNSELING PROGRAMS

Program Location	St:Co Ratio	Classroom Guidance											Small Group							Individual			Consultant				Coordination				Unique Component(s)
		Self-Concept	Self-Awareness	Study Skills	Decision Making	Communication	Interpersonal	Coping-Stress	Career	Testing	Substance Abuse	Personal Safety/Health	Peer Tutoring/Counseling	Student Development	Student Host	Special Needs	Motivation/School Attitudes	Attendance/"At Risk"	Interpersonal	Testing/Screening	Crisis Counseling	Special Needs	Parent	Teacher	Administration	Specialists	In-System Referral	Out-of-System Resources	School Testing/Screening	Evaluation of Program	
North Carolina																															
77. Durham [a] (S)	500:1	X	X			X							X			X				X		X	X				X				
78. Durham [b] (S/U)	380:1					X	X	X	X	X	X	X		X		X		X		X		X				X	X	X		X	Counselor Mentor Program
79. Greensboro (S)	500:1	X	X	X			X	X	X							X		X		X			X				X	X			
80. Winston-Salem (S)	625:1																						X	X							
North Dakota																															
81. Grand Forks (U)	600:1											X		X		X			X												
82. Minot (R)	578:1	X	X	X	X	X	X	X	X	X	X	X											X								

	Ratio															Notes
Ohio																
83. Dublin (S)	600:1	x					x		x	x						
84. Navarre (R/S)	1,200:1			x		x	x	x								Volunteers Provide Special Program
Oklahoma																
85. Moore (S)	400:1		x	x		x		x	x	x	x					
Oregon																
86. Oregon City (R/S)	350:1	x	x	x	x	x	x	x	x	x	x					Positive Addiction Groups: High Interest
87. Pendleton (R)	697:1		x x					x		x						
88. Portland (U)	350:1	x x	x x	x		x		x x								
89. Roseburg (R/S)	342:1	x	x	x		x	x									
90. Tigard (S)	450:1	x	x	x	x	x										
Pennsylvania																
91. Atglen (R)	950:1					x	x	x x	x							"PALS", "SMILE"
92. Carlisle (R)	225:1				x	x	x									
Puerto Rico																
93. Puerto Rico*	*							x								
South Carolina																
94. Batesburg (R)	1,100:1	x x			x		x x	x x	x	x	x					"GRIN", "Eaglet Eye"
95. Chapin (R)	950:1			x	x		x x									

U = Urban   S = Suburban   R = Rural   * = Unreported

MATRIX OF EXEMPLARY ELEMENTARY SCHOOL GUIDANCE AND COUNSELING PROGRAMS

Program Location	St:Co Ratio	Classroom Guidance											Small Group							Individual			Consultant				Coordination				Unique Component(s)
		Self-Concept	Self-Awareness	Study Skills	Decision Making	Communication	Interpersonal	Coping-Stress	Career	Testing	Substance Abuse	Personal Safety/Health	Peer Tutoring/Counseling	Student Development	Student Host	Special Needs	Motivation/School Attitudes	Attendance/"At Risk"	Interpersonal	Testing/Screening	Crisis Counseling	Special Needs	Parent	Teacher	Administration	Specialists	In-System Referral	Out-of-System Resources	School Testing/Screening	Evaluation of Program	
South Carolina (cont'd)																															
96. Columbia [a] (S)	500:1	X			X	X		X				X		X										X							
97. Columbia [b] (S)	1,150:1										X		X			X															
98. Columbia [c] (S)	600:1																				X		X	X				X		X	
99. Columbia [d] (S)	600:1					X	X	X				X	X		X						X		X	X							
100. Irmo (S)	790:1																						X								"Rainbow Room" Concept, Teacher Survival Kit, Teacher Coupon Book
South Dakota																															
101. Sioux Falls [a] (U)	850:1														X							X	X							X	

90

City	Ratio	...	"Indian Club" for Native Americans	"Success Express"	"Kids on the Block"	"Playroom" for Play Therapy	"Lunch Bunches"	Good Manners Clubs, Home Visits	Weekly Counselor Meetings	"GRIN" Folders	Developmental Characteristics Parent Booklet
102. Sioux Falls [b] (U)	780:1		x								
Tennessee											
103. Memphis (U)	1,100:1			x							
Texas											
104. Arlington (S)	1,515:1										
105. Irving (S)	625:1										
106. Katy (S)	730:1		x								
107. Richardson (S)	446:1		x								
108. San Antonio (U)	425:1		x		"Kids on the Block"						
Vermont											
109. Shelburne [a] (S)	350:1					"Playroom" for Play Therapy					
110. Shelburne [b] (S)	350:1										
111. Underhill (R)	365:1						"Lunch Bunches"				
Virginia											
112. Amherst (R)	750:1							Good Manners Clubs, Home Visits			
113. Harrisonburg (U)	600:1		x						Weekly Counselor Meetings		
114. Norfolk (U)	414:1									"GRIN" Folders	
115. Roanoke Co. (S)	423:1										Developmental Characteristics Parent Booklet

U = Urban   S = Suburban   R = Rural   * = Unreported

91

MATRIX OF EXEMPLARY ELEMENTARY SCHOOL GUIDANCE AND COUNSELING PROGRAMS

Program Location	St:Co Ratio	Classroom Guidance											Small Group							Individual			Consultant				Coordination				Unique Component(s)
		Self-Concept	Self-Awareness	Study Skills	Decision Making	Communication	Interpersonal	Coping-Stress	Career	Testing	Substance Abuse	Personal Safety/Health	Peer Tutoring/Counseling	Student Development	Student Host	Special Needs	Motivation/School Attitudes	Attendance/"At Risk"	Interpersonal	Testing/Screening	Crisis Counseling	Special Needs	Parent	Teacher	Administration	Specialists	In-System Referral	Out-of-System Resources	School Testing/Screening	Evaluation of Program	
Virginia (cont'd)																															
116. Staunton (U)	400:1	×	×				×		×							×							×	×							Parent Groups in Housing Developments, Cafeteria Mgr. Prepares Modified Lunches
117. Williamsburg [a] (S)	665:1										×					×							×				×	×		×	
118. Williamsburg [b] (S)	700:1										×					×		×					×				×	×		×	
119. Williamsburg [c] (S)	450:1						×	×	×		×					×							×	×						×	
Washington																															
120. Renton (S)	380:1	×	×		×		×	×	×				×			×														×	"Juvenile Jury"

92

West Virginia
121. Fairmont (U) — 700:1

Wisconsin
122. Appleton (U) — 700:1
123. Eau Claire (U/R) — 600:1
124. Menasha (U) — 390:1
125. New Berlin (S) — 325:1
126. Racine (U) — 700:1
127. Rhinelander (R) — 296:1
128. Sheboygan (U) — 414:1 — "Banana Split Group"
129. Sturgeon Bay (R) — 400:1
130. Waukesha (U) — 600:1
131. Waunakee (R) — 560:1 — Biofeedback/Self-Hypnosis for Relaxation

Wyoming
132. Douglas (R) — 436:1
133. Glenrock (R) — 300:1
134. Rock Spring (R) — 400:1

U = Urban   S = Suburban   R = Rural   * = Unreported

93

INTO THE FUTURE

What were some of the views of participants about this conference designed to showcase exemplary elementary school guidance and counseling programs from across the United States? Did the conference meet the needs of all participants? Did ratings differ by type of position held or by area of residence of the participant? What kind of emphasis did participants want for conferences in the future?

In order to answer these questions a 25-item evaluation form was developed by the project research director and distributed to conference participants in their packet of materials. This one-page form was designed to elicit perceptions of conference effectiveness, usefulness, and applicability. It appears in the appendix as Figure 6. Participants were asked to complete the one-page form and return it at the close of the conference. Responses were received from 219 (55%) of those attending the conference, a high percentage for this type of evaluation.

Conference respondents represented many school divisions nationwide. Forty-one percent said that counselors were required in their elementary schools, either by district, division, county, or state mandate. Twenty-five percent were from school divisions that had elementary school counselors, although they were not required. Twenty-three percent were in school divisions that did not have elementary school counselors but expected to have them within 1 to 2 years. This distribution is probably somewhat skewed for the country as a whole and probably reflects the current mandate in Virginia that requires an elementary counselor for every 500 children.

Although the conference had representation from a wide range of geographic areas, (one individual came from as far as Alaska), the location at
Blacksburg, Virginia, in rural southwest Virginia made it difficult for people
outside of the state of Virginia to attend. Not surprisingly, 75% of those
in attendance were from Virginia, and the remaining group was equally
divided between those from the bordering states to Virginia (West Virginia,
Kentucky, Tennessee, Maryland, and North Carolina) and those beyond
the border region.

The conference received very high overall ratings. In response to the
question: What overall rating would you give this conference? 96% of
respondents rated the conference either excellent or good. Clearly, the
conference was viewed positively by almost all respondents. This was true
regardless of the position they held in their educational programs. One
hundred percent of principals, college professors, and professionals working at the state or central office levels rated the conference highly as did
97% of students, 95% of elementary school counselors, 94% of teachers,
and 92% of supervisors.

Did the conference meet the differential needs of participants depend-
ing on their position? In general the answer to the question was yes, with
more than 90% of teachers, students, principals, supervisors, and college
professors evaluating the conference either as excellent or good. Elementary counselors rated this question slightly lower (84%). Their comments to open-ended questions reflected a desire to have had sessions
devoted to more advanced material.

Did the conference differentially meet the needs of participants de-
pending on their geographic location? In general the answer to this question was also yes, although those from states other than Virginia or a
border state gave somewhat lower ratings to the quality of presentations
than did the other two groups. Table 4.1 gives ratings by location.

TABLE 4.1

Percentage of Excellent or Good Ratings by Area of Residence

Statement	Virginia	Border State	Other
Overall Rating	95	96	100
Quality of Presentation	91	100	82
Usefulness of Information	91	100	93
Applicability for Needs	87	100	100
Effectiveness of Presenters	89	96	89

How did the respondents describe the conference? We selected terms that might be used to indicate feelings about the conference and asked respondents to rate these using a Likert-scale format. Data from these ratings are given in Table 4.2.

The need, importance, and timeliness of such a conference are clearly demonstrated by the extremely high percentage of respondents who rated these dimensions "considerably." Other terms that were rated "considerably" or "usually" by a high percentage of respondents were educational, thought-provoking, challenging, innovative, and exciting. Conversely, only a few thought the conference was unfocused, boring, or controversial.

Did respondents want future conferences and what topics did they want to see represented? Eighty-five percent of respondents replied in the affirmative when asked if they wanted another conference. (Would you attend a conference next year?) Only 4% responded that they would not attend a future conference.

TABLE 4.2

Feelings About the Conference

	Considerably	Usually	Somewhat	Not Very
	Percent Responding*			
Needed	90	8	2	1
Important	82	13	4	—
Timely	78	13	4	3
Educational	73	20	6	1
Thought-provoking	63	27	7	2
Challenging	50	30	13	7
Exciting	48	32	17	3
Innovative	46	39	12	3
Entertaining	21	44	27	7
Boring	4	2	16	79
Controversial	7	2	27	6
Unfocused	6	1	5	89

*May not total 100% due to omissions or rounding.

Types of future program topics suggested by participants varied, but the primary focus reflected a desire to attend a conference that emphasized professional development and, in particular, the development of specific counseling skills for individual and group work. Counselors are asking for help in technique development.

Graduate students in counseling at Virginia Tech who participated in the data analysis of the conference evaluation as part of a research course were Charlene Doss of Pulaski County, Virginia Public Schools, Victor Edwards of Giles County, Virginia Public Schools, and Janet Morgan of the Wythe County Virginia Public School system. We want to thank them for their help and insightful recommendations.

CONCLUSIONS

Several important observations drawn from our experience in conducting this project, participating in each phase, evaluating the outcome, and planning activities for the future should be mentioned.

First, it is very clear that the elementary school guidance and counseling programs we learned about have a strong, easily identified comprehensive developmental focus. They operate along preventive lines (as opposed to remedial), and group counseling activities are utilized frequently. What is less clear is the incorporation of a result or student-outcome basis of evaluation. Although some programs reference an outcome or product measurement of their efforts in their written program descriptions and some even demonstrate how they do it, we cannot yet say that outcome evaluation has been established by more than a few of these exemplary programs. School counselors, guidance supervisors, and counselor educators need to work harder to make outcome-based guidance a reality in the elementary schools.

Second, further efforts need to be made to inform our various publics, both professional and lay, of the meaning of comprehensive/developmental/outcome-oriented elementary school counseling and specifically how counseling is different from other helping models, particularly school social work and school psychology. The crisis intervention model and the "assess and adjust the student in need of remedial help" model remain the general notion of what the elementary school counselor does by too many significant and influential persons in public education. Counselors may see themselves as operating out of a developmental model, but it is most important that colleagues, supervisors, parents, and others in the public see it as well.

A third point to underscore is this. We received nearly 200 nominations of programs thought to be of exemplary quality by persons with excellent credentials to know. Consequently, we are sure that the listing of the nominees that appears in the appendix of this document is an elite array of high quality guidance programs. We encourage individuals who are committed to the improvement of their efforts to network with the leaders of these programs. We are, however, struck by the absence of representation from our largest public school districts in our major cities, with few exceptions. Surely there are exemplary programs in elementary school counseling in these important communities. It is suggested that there is a need to target, identify, and disseminate what is exemplary in big city elementary school guidance.

Fourth, we suggest that partnership models between school districts, universities, and state education agencies are the necessary alliances if new counselor training program models are to take hold. University training is the foundation and the source of each generation of elementary school counselors. Areas of professional concern frequently reflect a lack of agreement among authorities, and this is not a time for school districts, state education offices, and counselor training institutions to go it alone. The task of the decade of the 1990s seems, therefore, to be one of working out a partnership model on issues in three broad categories:

1. Agree on the assumptions and conditions necessary to establish outcome evaluation as a part of comprehensive developmental elementary school guidance.
2. Delineate clearly the personnel and procedures needed—the division of labor between teacher-counselor-psychologist-social worker and other pupil personnel workers.
3. Program elementary guidance activities as an integral part of the curriculum in the public schools.

A professional association has many important functions. Our common goal of the best for our kids must be met. In support of elementary counseling, ASCA should be in the forefront of encouraging improved professional development and practice. It should provide support to those who are working to improve the techniques and tools of counseling. And it should provide leadership to those with a vision for the future. We are confident that ASCA will meet these challenges.

References

Dinkmeyer, D. (1966). Developmental counseling in the elementary school. *Personnel and Guidance Journal, 45*, 262–266.

Faust, V. (1968). *History of elementary school counseling: Overview and critique.* Boston: Houghton Mifflin.

Gerstein, M. (1989). Exemplary programs in elementary school counselor preparation: A consortium approach. *Virginia Counselors Journal, 17*, 46–52.

Guilford County School System. (1985). *The school guidance and counseling resource manual K–5.* Greensboro, NC: Author.

Gysbers, N.C., & Henderson, P. (1988). *Developing and managing your school guidance program.* Alexandria, VA: AACD.

Hoffman, L. (1989). Elementary counselors in Virginia: Past, present and future. *Virginia Counselors Journal, 17*, 35–45.

Hollis, J.W., & Wantz, R.A. (1986). *Counselor preparation 1986–89: Programs, personnel trends.* Muncie, IN: Accelerated Development.

Iowa Department of Education. (1986). *Iowa K–12 career guidance curriculum guide for student development.* Des Moines, IA: Author.

Lake County, Florida, Public Schools. (1985). *Schoolwide experiences in affective learning, SEAL patrol.* Tavarres, FL: Author.

Lewis, J. (1983). Guidance program evaluation: How to do it. *The School Counselor, 31*, 111–119.

Menasha Joint School District. (1983). *Menasha developmental guidance curriculum.* Menasha, WI: Author.

Myrick, R.D. (1987). *Developmental guidance and counseling: A practical approach.* Minneapolis: Educational Media Corporation.

North Carolina Department of Public Instruction. (1985). *Teacher handbook: Guidance K–12 subject by subject. North Carolina competency based curriculum.* Raleigh, NC: Author.

Osseo-Fairchild School District. (1984). *Osseo-Fairchild developmental guidance curriculum.* Osseo, WI: Author.

Racine Unified School District. (1984). *SGS student guidance system grades K–12. Developmental guidance and counseling.* Racine, WI: Author.

Shaw, M.C., & Tuel, J.K. (1966). A focus for public school guidance programs: A model and proposal. *Personnel and Guidance Journal, 44*, 824–830.

Sioux Falls School District 49–5. (date unavailable). *Developmental guidance and counseling plan for kindergarten through sixth grade.* Sioux Falls, SD: Author.

Uhl, N.P. (1971). Identifying institutional goals: Encouraging convergence of opinion through the delphi technique. *NLHE Research Monograph Number Two.* Durham, NC: National Laboratory for Higher Education.

Winneconne Community School District. (1988). *Winneconne developmental guidance curriculum*. Winneconne, WI: Author.

Wisconsin Department of Public Instruction. (1986). *School counseling programs: A resource and planning guide*. Madison: Author.

Additional Resources and References

The resources that appear below are referred to in the program descriptions throughout this text. They are illustrative of available resources for use in elementary school guidance and counseling. This is not, however, intended to be a comprehensive list. Further, the resources have not been evaluated by, nor are they endorsed or recommended by, the authors, the American School Counselor Association, or the American Association for Counseling and Development.

Allan, J., & Anderson, E. (1986). Children and crisis: A classroom guidance approach. *Elementary School Guidance and Counseling, 21*, 143–149.

Allan, J., & Bardsley, P. (1983). Transient children in the elementary school: A group counseling approach. *The School Counselor, 35*, 162–169.

Allred, C. (1983). *Positive action*. Twin Falls, ID: Positive Action Publishing.

Arena, C., Hermann, J., & Hoffman, T. (1984). Helping children deal with the death of a classmate: A crisis intervention model. *Elementary School Guidance and Counseling 19*, 107–115.

Blair, J., Marchant, K., & Medway, F. (1984). Aiding the relocated family and mobile child. *Elementary School Guidance and Counseling, 18*, 251–259.

Brookshire, M., & Noland, M. (1985). Teaching children about death. *Elementary School Guidance and Counseling, 20*, 74–79.

Brown, J.A. (1977). *Organizing and evaluating elementary school guidance services: Why, what and how*. Monterey, CA: Brooks/Cole.

Bruckner, S., & Thompson, C., (1987). Guidance program evaluation: An example. *Elementary School Guidance and Counseling, 21*, 193–196.

Bundy, M. (1986). Coping with change: A guidance unit. *Elementary School Guidance and Counseling, 20*, 297–302.

California State Department of Education. (1987). *Program quality review for counseling and guidance*. Sacramento, CA: Author.

Cantrell, R. (1986). Adjustment to divorce: Three components to assist children. *Elementary School Guidance and Counseling, 20*, 163–173.

Clark, R., & Firth, G. (1983). Writing a developmental counseling curriculum: The Vestavia Hills experience. *The School Counselor, 30,* 292–298.

Commonwealth of Virginia. Department of Education. (1983). *A guide for planning and developing guidance and counseling programs in Virginia's public schools.* Richmond, VA: Author.

Dagley, J. (1987). A new look at developmental guidance: The hearthstone of school counseling. *The School Counselor, 35,* 102–109.

Dinkmeyer, D., & Dinkmeyer, D., Jr. *DUSO-R. Developing understanding of self and others.* Circle Pines, MN: American Guidance Service.

Dupont, H., Gardner, O.S., & Brody, D.S. (1974). *TAD Toward affective development.* Circle Pines: MN: American Guidance Service.

Edwards, D.M., & Zander, T. (1985). Children of alcoholics: Background and strategies for the counselor. *Elementary School Guidance and Counseling, 20,* 121–128.

Elliott, S. (1987). The emotional barometer: A graphic aid to counseling. *Elementary School Guidance and Counseling, 21,* 312–317.

Goldberg, L. (1983). *Counseling activities for children of alcoholics.* Tallahassee, FL: Apalachee Community Mental Health Services, Inc.

Gysbers, N.C., & Moore, E.J. (1981). *Improving guidance programs.* Englewood Cliffs, NJ: Prentice-Hall.

Hammond, J. (1981). *Group counseling for children of divorce: A guide for elementary school.* Flint, MI: Cranbrook Publishing Co.

Hargens, M., & Gysbers, N.C. (1984). How to remodel a guidance program while living in it: A case study. *The School Counselor, 32,* 119–125.

Herr, E.L. (1979). *Guidance and counseling in the schools: The past, present, and future.* Washington, DC: APGA.

Hitchcock, R., & Young, D. (1986). Prevention of sexual assault: A curriculum for elementary school counselors. *Elementary School Guidance and Counseling, 20,* 201–207.

Landy, L. (1984). *Child support (through small group counseling).* Savannah: GA: Lois Landy Publisher.

Lichtman, M., Barokas, J., Kaplan, S., & Royeen, C. (1989). Distributions of variables in clinical research. In C.B. Royeen (Ed.), *Clinical research handbook* (pp. 1–28). New Jersey: Slack Inc.

Lisko, S., & Ferdinande, G. (1984). *Families in change. Facilitator's handbook.* Rochester, MN: Rochester Public Schools.

Myer, R., James, D., & Street, T. (1987). Counseling internationally adopted children: A classroom meeting approach. *Elementary School Guidance and Counseling, 22,* 88–94.

Myrick, R.D., & Bowman, R.P. (1981). *Children helping children: Teaching students to become friendly helpers.* Minneapolis, MN: Educational Media Corp.

Nelson, R. (1987). Graphics in counseling. *Elementary School Guidance and Counseling, 22,* 17–29.

Practical ideas for counselors. Doylestown, PA: *Marco.* (A newsletter for elementary and middle school counselors.)

Tedder, S., Scherman, A., & Wantz, R. (1987). Effectiveness of a support group for children of divorce. *Elementary School Guidance and Counseling, 22,* 102–109.

Thompson, C.L., & Rudolph, L.B. (1988). *Counseling children.* (2nd ed.). Monterey, CA: Brooks/Cole.

Toenniessen, C., Little, L., & Rosen, K. (1985). Anybody home? Evaluation and intervention techniques with latchkey children. *Elementary School Guidance and Counseling, 20,* 105–113.

Wilson, N.H. (1982). Evaluation tools: A sampler. *Elementary School Guidance and Counseling, 17,* 61–65.

Selected Publishers' and School Division Addresses

American Guidance Service
Publishers' Building
P.O. Box 99
Circle Pines, MN 55014

Apalachee Center for Human
  Services
P.O. Box 1782
Tallahassee, FL 32302

Cranbrook Publishing Company
2302 Windemere
Flint, MI 48053

Educational Media Corporation
Box 21311
Minneapolis, MN 55421

Growing Up
22 N. Second Street
P.O. Box 620
Lafayette, IN 47902

Guilford County Schools
Guidance Services
120 Franklin Blvd.
Greensboro, NC 27401

Iowa Department of Education
Guidance Services
Grimes State Office Building
Des Moines, IA 50319

Lake County Schools
Lee Educational Center
207 North Lee Street
Leesburg, FL 32748

Learning Tree Filmstrips
P.O. Box 4116
Englewood, CO 80155

Lois Landy Publisher
204 Maria Road
Savannah, GA 31410

Marco
P.O. Box 1052
Doylestown, PA 18901

Menasha Joint School District
449 Ahnaip Street
P.O. Box 360
Menasha, WI 54952

North Carolina Department of
  Public Instruction
Publication Sales
116 West Edenton Street
Raleigh, NC 27603

Osseo-Fairchild Schools
13th and Francis Street
Osseo, WI 54758

Paperbacks for Educators
1240 Ridge Road
Ballwin, MO 63021

Positive Action Publishing
321 Eastland Drive
P.O. Box 2347
Twin Falls, ID 83303

Racine Unified School District
2220 Northwestern Avenue
Racine, WI 53404

Rochester Public Schools
ISD #535
Educational Services Center
334 S.E. 16th Street
Rochester, MN 55904

Sunburst Communications
101 Castleton Street
Pleasantville, NY 10570

Winneconne Community School
    District
233 South Third Avenue
Winneconne, WI 54986

Wisconsin Department of Public
    Instruction
Publications Sales Office
125 S. Webster Street
P.O. Box 7841
Madison, WI 53707

APPENDIX

A RESOURCE NETWORK OF EXEMPLARY ELEMENTARY SCHOOL COUNSELING PROGRAMS

ALABAMA

Auburn City Board of Education
Anita Hardin
Supervisor of Guidance
P.O. Box 2208
Auburn, AL 36830
(205) 887-2100

Wrights Mill Road Elementary
  School
School Counselor
P.O. Box 2336
Auburn, AL 36831
(205) 887-2147, 48

Gwin Elementary School
Barbara Mayer
School Counselor
1580 Patton Chapel Road
Birmingham, AL 35226
(205) 822-0966

Huntsville Public Schools
Teri J. Stokes
Elementary Supervisor
P.O. Box 1256
Huntsville, AL 35807
(205) 532-4718

Russell County Public Schools
Bertha M. Dansby
Elementary Supervisor
P.O. Box 67
Seale, AL 36875
(205) 855-4721

Tarrant Elementary School
School Counselor
1269 Portland Street
Tarrant, AL 35217
(205) 841-7544

Tuscaloosa City Schools
Barbara C. Adams
School Counselor
1100 21st Street East
Tuscaloosa, AL 35405
(205) 759-3700

Vestavia Hills School System
Reba Clark
Director of Guidance
1204 Montgomery Highway
Vestavia Hills, AL 35216
(205) 823-0295

ARKANSAS

Thomas Jefferson Elementary and
  Bentonville Kindergarten Center
  Counseling Program
Brenda Fuller and Jamey Chitwood
Counselors
810 Bella Vista Rd.
Bentonville, AR 72712
(501) 273-3339

Conway Public Schools
Carolyn Scott
Supervisor of Guidance and
  Counseling
Administration Building
Hwy. 60 West
Conway, AR 72032
(501) 329-5638

Newark Elementary School
Koletta Duncan
School Counselor
P.O. Box 336
Newark, AR 72562
(501) 799-8691

Springdale Public Schools
Richard Louis DeWitt
Counselor
1102 West Emma
Springdale, AR 72764
(501) 751-4838

Wynne Intermediate School
Sue Hull
School Counselor
P.O. Box 69
Wynne, AR 72396
(501) 238-2636

CALIFORNIA

Ceres Counseling Center
Eldon F. De Witt
Director Pupil Personnel
2503 Lawrence Street
Ceres, CA 95307
(209) 538-0145

Ceres Unified School District
Virginia Lish
Curriculum Specialist
P.O. Box 307
Ceres, CA 95307
(209) 538-0148

Newport-Mesa Unified School
  District
Carrie Eggleston
Director Project Launch
425 E. 18th Street
Costa Mesa, CA 92627
(714) 760-3404

Glendora Unified School District
Sheila Gutierrez
Guidance Consultant
352 N. Wabash Avenue
Glendora, CA 91740
(213) 961-1611

Long Beach Unified School District
Winifred Strong
Elementary Supervisor of Guidance
701 Locust Avenue
Long Beach, CA 90813
(213) 436-9931

San Diego Unified School District
Chris Pare
District Counselor Supervisor
Guidance Services Department
5650 Mt. Ackerly Drive
San Diego, CA 92111
(619) 560-7505

Parklane Elementary School
Lodi Unified School District
Christy Reinhold
School Counselor
8405 Tam O'Shanter
Stockton, CA 95210
(209) 953-8410

COLORADO

Vaughn School
Sandy Darby
School Counselor
1155 Vaughn
Aurora, CO 80011
(303) 366-8430

Dunn/Washington Elementary
    School
Julie B. Wertz
School Counselor
501 S. Washington Street
Ft. Collins, CO 82526
(303) 482-0450

Platte Valley Elementary School
Douglas J. Neihart
School Counselor
P.O. Box 487
Kersey, CO 80644
(303) 463-5650

Gilcrest Elementary School
Loretta Purtill
Elementary/Middle School
    Counselor
P.O. Box 427
Platteville, CO 80651
(303) 737-2409

CONNECTICUT

F.A. Berry School
Helen W. Chapman
School Counselor and K–12
    Coordinator
Whittlesey Drive
Bethel, CT 06801
(203) 794-8677

DELAWARE

Milford School District
John B. Caldwell
School Counselor
906 Lakeview Avenue
Milford, DE 19963
(302) 422-1630, 40

Carrie Downie Elementary School
Betty DeBoer
School Counselor
Frenchtown Road
New Castle, DE 19720
(302) 323-2929

West Seaford Elementary School
Diane Huffman
School Counselor
Sussex Avenue
Seaford, DE 19973
(302) 629-9352

DISTRICT OF COLUMBIA

D.C. Public Schools
Group Counseling Program
Vida Usilton
Liaison
Room 906, 415 12th Street, N.W.
Washington, DC 20004
(202) 724-4185

D.C. Public Schools
Parent Education Program
Elaine Black
Coordinator
Room 906, 415 12th Street, N.W.
Washington, DC 20004
(202) 724-4185

D.C. Public Schools
Peer Counseling Program Model
John W. Porter
Elementary Supervisor
Room 906, 415 12th Street, N.W.
Washington, DC 20004
(202) 724-4185

J.O. Wilson Elementary School
Geralyn Wicker
School Counselor
6th and K Streets, N.E.
Washington, DC 20002
(202) 724-4707

FLORIDA

Glen Springs Elementary School
Marjorie I. Cuthbert
School Counselor
2826 N.W. 31st Avenue
Gainesville, FL 32605
(904) 336-2708

J.J. Finley Elementary School
Mary Anne Wagner
School Counselor

1912 N.W. 5th Avenue
Gainesville, FL 32603
(904) 336-2705

Metcalf Elementary School
Cindy Campbell
School Counselor
1905 N.E. 12th Street
Gainesville, FL 32609
(904) 336-2713

Newberry Elementary School
Jack Carter
School Counselor
P.O. Box 498
Newberry, FL 32669
(904) 472-2144

Lake Como Elementary
   Guidance Program
Karen Lynn Mittlemark
School Counselor
901 S. Bumby Avenue
Orlando, FL 32806
(407) 894-0401

Orange County Public Schools
Elementary Guidance Supervisor
434 N. Tampa Avenue
Orlando, FL 32805
(407) 423-9244

Pinar Elementary School
Nancy R. Allen
School Counselor
3701 Anthony Lane
Orlando, FL 32822
(407) 277-6360

Shenandoah Elementary School
Carolyn S. Peterson
School Counselor
4827 South Conway Road
Orlando, FL 32812
(407) 855-8431

Belle Witter Elementary School
Gwen Drapela
School Counselor
10801 N. 22nd Street
Tampa, FL 33612
(813) 971-6721

Woodbridge Elementary School
Judith Louise Channing
School Counselor
8301 Woodbridge Blvd.
Tampa, FL 33615
(813) 886-2945

GEORGIA

Glyndale Elementary School
Joanne Higginbotham
School Counselor
711 Old Jessup Road
Brunswick, GA 31502
(912) 264-8740

Sugar Hill Elementary School
James A. Harrison
School Counselor
1160 Level Creek Road
Buford, GA 30518
(404) 945-5735, 2375

Forsyth County Public Schools
Bobbie Overton and Sally Curry
School Counselors
101 School Street
Cumming, GA 30130
(404) 887-2461

Whitfield County Public Schools
Henry L. Cooper
Director of Student Services
1306 S. Thornton Avenue
Dalton, GA 30720
(404) 278-8070

Douglas County Public Schools
Janice G. Rollins
Coordinator of Counseling and
    Guidance
8334 Connally Drive
P.O. Box 1077
Douglasville, GA 30133
(404) 942-5411

Gwinnett County Public Schools
James D. Wiggins
Coordinator of Counseling and
    Guidance
52 Gwinnett Drive
Lawrenceville, GA 30278
(404) 962-1384

Chatham County Public Schools
Diane Paxman
Supervisor of Guidance and
    Counseling
208 Bull Street
Savannah, GA 31401
(912) 651-7270

HAWAII

Honolulu District, DOE
State of Hawaii
Kenneth A. Omura
District Education Specialist
4967 Kilanea Avenue
Honolulu, HI 96816
(808) 735-1796

Nanakuli Elementary School
Edward Kawamoto
School Counselor
89-778 Haleakala Avenue
Waianae, HI 96792
(808) 668-2939, 49

Hawaii *Continued*

Nanaikapono Elementary School
Clara Burrows
School Counselor
89-195 Farrington Highway
Waianae, HI 96792
(808) 668-1151

IDAHO

Boise Public Schools
Caren Reese
Supervisor
1207 Fort Street
Boise, ID 83702
(208) 338-3600, 80

ILLINOIS

Douglas Elementary School
Janet Schloemann
School Counselor
125 Carlyle
Belleville, IL 62220
(618) 233-2417

Bloomington School District
School Counselor
Oakland School
1605 E. Oakland Avenue
Bloomington, IL 61701
(309) 662-4302

Havana Junior High School
Donna Sisson
School Counselor
Rt. 136 East
Havana, IL 62644
(309) 543-6677

INDIANA

William Reed School
Nancy Barry
School Counselor
202 E. Chestnut Street
Hartford City, IN 47807
(317) 348-0600

Hoagland Elementary School
Melanie K. Scheumann
School Counselor
12009 Hoagland Road
Hoagland, IN 46745
(219) 639-3212, 6514

La Porte Community Schools
Hailman Elementary/Crichfield
    Elementary Schools
Sally Mayes
School Counselor
336 W. Johnson Road
La Porte, IN 46350
(219) 362-2020

Charles Elementary School
Barbara A. Blake
School Counselor
2400 Reeveston Road
Richmond, IN 47374
(317) 962-7104

Deming Elementary School
Donna Wernz
School Counselor
1750 Eighth Avenue
Terre Haute, IN 47804
(812) 238-4431, 93

IOWA

West Des Moines Community
  Schools
Catherine G. Stjernberg
Chairperson
Guidance Department
8355 Franklin Avenue
Des Moines, IA 50322
(515) 276-8116

Ballard Community School
Carolyn McCall
School Counselor
315 Main Street
Huxley, IA 50124
(515) 597-2811

Nevada Community School
Judy Strohbehn
School Counselor
9th Street and I Avenue
Nevada, IA 50201
(515) 382-2383

KANSAS

Burlington Lower Elementary
  School
Julia D. Elson
School Counselor
626 Niagara Street
Burlington, KS 66801
(316) 364-6882

Council Grove Elementary School
Cindy Schultz
School Counselor
706 E. Main Street
Council Grove, KS 66846
(316) 767-6851

Dodge City Public Schools
Ethel Peterson
School Counselor
Sunnyside Elementary School
511 Sunnyside Avenue
Dodge City, KS 67801
(316) 227-6701

Walnut Elementary School
Susie Bond
School Counselor
801 Grove
Emporia, KS 66801
(316) 342-6077

Manhattan Middle School
Wanda Clark
School Counselor
901 Poyntz Avenue
Manhattan, KS 66502
(913) 537-0240

Olathe Public Schools
Jeanene Hatcher Camp
Coordinator of Counseling
905 N. Walker/1021 S. Pitt
Olathe, KS 66061
(913) 764-1770, 782-6111

KENTUCKY

Goshen Elementary School
School Counselor
Box 116
Goshen, KY 40026
(502) 228-0101

Bates Elementary School
Shirley Fuqua-Jackson
School Counselor
7601 Bardstown Road
Louisville, KY 40291
(502) 454-8208

LOUISIANA

East Baton Rouge Parish School
  Board
Betty K. Addison
Supervisor of Guidance and
  Counseling
P.O. Box 2950
Baton Rouge, LA 70821
(504) 922-5443

Louisiana *Continued*

Lafayette Parish Schools
Betty D. Cooper
Supervisor of Guidance and
    Counseling
P.O. Drawer 2158
Lafayette, LA 70502
(318) 236-6867

B.M. Palmer Elementary School
Helen Castenell
School Counselor
1339 Clout Street
New Orleans, LA 70117
(504) 945-2060

G.W. Carver Middle School
Percie Ann Rodney and McMorris A.
    Whitfield
School Counselors
3019 Higgins Blvd.
New Orleans, LA 70126
(504) 945-0826

Phyllis Wheatley Elementary School
Brenda Williams
School Counselor
2300 Dumaine Street
New Orleans, LA 70019
(504) 822-4782

Caddo Middle Magnet School
Kay Robinson and Louise Jones
School Counselors
7635 Cornelious Drive
Shreveport, LA 71106
(318) 869-3038

South Highlands Elementary Magnet
    for the Performing Arts
Judy Livingston and Susie Jefferson
School Counselors
831 Erie Street
Shreveport, LA 71106
(318) 865-5119

MAINE

Fairview-Stevens Mills School
Carl Bucciantini
School Counselor
Minot Avenue
Auburn, ME 04210
(207) 784-3559

G. Herbert Jewett School
Charlotte B. White
School Counselor
Bucksport, ME 04416
(207) 469-3013

MARYLAND

Anne Arundel County Public Schools
C.D. Johnson
Supervisor of Guidance and
    Counseling
2644 Riva Road
Annapolis, MD 21401
(301) 224-5280

MASSACHUSETTS

Fort River Elementary School
Mary Bradford Ivey
School Counselor
70 South East Street
Amherst, MA 01002
(413) 253-9731

Belmont Public Schools
William Brogna
Director
221 Concord Avenue
Belmont, MA 02178
(617) 484-6175

Hawlemont Regional School
Gordon Parker and Siv Sandberg
School Counselors
School Street
Charlemont, MA 01339
(413) 339-8316

Elementary School Union #38
Susan Hagberg
School Counselor
311 Main Street
So. Deerfield, MA 01373
(413) 665-4866

Bennett Hemingway School
Carol Van Cleave
School Counselor
East Evergreen Road
Natick, MA 01760
(617) 651-7198

Natick Public Schools
Marilou Cashman
Director
13 E. Central Street
Natick, MA 01760
(617) 651-7115

MINNESOTA

Meadowbrook Elementary School
Dennis Haversack
School Counselor
5430 Glenwood Avenue
Golden Valley, MN 55422
(612) 933-9364

Washington School
Judy Olson Mosca
School Counselor
910 North 14th Street
New Ulm, MN 56073
(507) 359-8490

Northfield Public Schools
Douglas C. Peterson
School Counselor
401 Juniper Avenue West
Northfield, MN 55057
(507) 663-0670

Pine Island Elementary School
Kate Flynn
School Counselor
P.O. Box 398
Pine Island, MN 55963
(507) 356-8581

Jefferson Elementary School
Jane V. Bogan
School Counselor
1210 N.E. 10th Avenue
Rochester, MN 55904
(507) 281-6091

MISSISSIPPI

Walls Elementary School
Susan Eubanks
School Counselor
6131 Delta View Road
Walls, MS 38680
(601) 781-1280

MISSOURI

Humboldt Elementary School
Judith K. Fuston
School Counselor
1604 N. 2nd Street
St. Joseph, MO 64505
(806) 232-0744

MONTANA

Missoula District One
Mike Vance
Assistant Superintendent
215 S. 6th West
Missoula, MT 59801
(406) 728-4000

Stevensville Schools
Peggy Mallette
School Counselor
Stevensville, MT 59870
(406) 777-5533

NEBRASKA

Park School
Julie A. Dinsmore
School Counselor
310 West 24th Street
Kearney, NE 58847
(308) 237-2985

Prairie View Elementary School
Linda S. Lund
School Counselor
801 East O
Ogallala, NE 69153
(308) 284-6087

Millard Public Schools
Dennis Harding
Director of Pupil Personnel Services
13270 Millard Avenue
Omaha, NE 68137
(402) 895-8300

Pleasanton Public Schools
Bob Bedner
School Counselor
303 W. Church Street
Pleasanton, NE 68866
(308) 388-2041

NEVADA

Oran Grayson Elementary School
Janet Duhaney
School Counselor
555 N. Honolulu
Las Vegas, NV 89110
(702) 799-7330

Florence Drake Elementary School
Betty Barker
Program Assistant in Counseling
2755 4th Street
Sparks, NV 89431
(702) 358-2691

NEW MEXICO

West Las Vegas Schools
Conchita M. Montano
Substance Abuse Prevention
    Director
179 Bridge Street
Las Vegas, NM 87701
(505) 425-7511

NEW YORK

North Park Academy #66
Florence Rozier
School Counselor
Tacoma/Parkside
Buffalo, NY 14216
(716) 838-2398

Shenendehowa Central School
    District
Gregory Georgelos
Director
Guidance and Pupil Personnel
    Services
1 Fairchild Square
Clifton Park, NY 12065
(518) 877-6251

Little Britain Elementary School
Joyce Anderson
School Counselor
Box 97, Rd 2, Rte. 207
Newburgh, NY 12550
(914) 496-9111, 561-4207

Sidney Central Schools
Emily Phillips
School Counselor
Pearl Street
Sidney, NY 13838
(607) 563-4202

Townsend Elementary School
Valerie Vogel
School Counselor
North Street
Walton, NY 13856
(607) 865-4116

NORTH CAROLINA

Durham County Schools
Elizabeth Moore Feifs
Director of Student Services
P.O. Box 3823
Durham, NC 27702
(919) 683-2591

Hillandale Elementary School
Geoff Wyckoff and Laura Swanson
School Counselors
2107 Hillandale Road
Durham, NC 27705
(919) 477-4452

Guilford County School System
Eleanor Yoder
Coordinator of Guidance Services
120 Franklin Blvd.
Greensboro, NC 27402
(919) 271-0666

Powell Elementary School
Sandy Pearce
School Counselor
1130 Marlborough Road
Raleigh, NC 27610
(919) 755-6607

Hunter Elementary School
Mary Moseley
School Counselor
1018 E. Davie
Raleigh, NC 27601
(919) 755-6362

Wake County Schools
Ronald Anderson
School Counselor
Box 28041
Raleigh, NC 27611
(919) 790-2300

Old Town School
School Counselor
3930 Reynolda Road
Winston-Salem, NC 27106
(919) 924-9246

Winston-Salem Public Schools
William Albright
School Counselor
Box 2513
Winston-Salem, NC 27102
(919) 727-2816

NORTH DAKOTA

Grand Forks Public School
Frank Miller
Director of Guidance and
   Counseling
911 Cottonwood Street
Grand Forks, ND 58201
(701) 746-2230

North Dakota *Continued*

Dakota Elementary, MAFB
Jeff Lofthus
School Counselor
215 2nd Street
Minot, ND 58701
(701) 727-6306

OHIO

Moler Elementary School
Carol Thomas Rivers
School Counselor
1560 Moler Street
Columbus, OH 43207
(614) 444-1131

Riverside Elementary School
Lisa A. Shannon
School Counselor
3260 Riverside Green
Dublin, OH 43017
(604) 764-5940

Perry Local Schools
Lohr Elementary School
Tommie Radd
Guidance Coordinator and School
   Counselor
5300 Richville Drive SW
Navarre, OH 44662
(216) 484-3924

OKLAHOMA

Moore Public Schools
Pat Ross
Supervisor of Guidance and
   Counseling
2009 North Janeway
Moore, OK 73160
(405) 794-8282, 1874

Pioneer Intermediate School
Sandi McCoy
School Counselor
Box 579
Noble, OK 73068
(405) 972-3472

Wewoka Elementary School
I. Claudean Hurley
School Counselor
Box 870
Wewoka, OK 74884
(405) 257-3751

OREGON

Oregon City Schools
Marian Lee
School Counselor
13521 S. Gaffney Lane
Oregon City, OR 97045
(503) 657-2441

Umatilla County Education Service
   District
Richard R. Huston
Coordinator
Child Development Specialist
   Program
412 S.E. Dorian Avenue
Pendleton, OR 97801
(503) 276-6616

Portland Public Schools
Carolyn Sheldon
Assistant Director
Student Services
Roselyn Taylor
Coordinator
Child Development Specialist
   Program
8020 NE Tillamook
Portland, OR 97213
(503) 280-5790

Douglas County School District 4
Dennis L. Acton
Director of Elementary Education
1419 NW Valley View Drive
Roseburg, OR 97470
(503) 440-4010

Salem Keizer Public Schools
Marilyn Herb
School Counselor
P.O. Box 12024
Salem, OR 97309
(503) 399-3101

Tigard School District
Sharon Parker
School Counselor
12615 S.W. 72nd
Tigard, OR 97223
(503) 684-2318

PENNSYLVANIA

Octorara Elementary School
Beverly B. Kahn
School Counselor
Box 65-A
Atglen, PA 19310
(215) 593-8242

Trinity Area School District
Robert L. Cimino
Guidance Department
  Representative
99 Manse Street
Washington, PA 15301
(412) 225-7490

PUERTO RICO

Region Educativa de San Juan
Blanca Mawad
Guidance Counseling Supervisor
Hato Ray, PR 00919
(809) 758-4221, 762-2202

SOUTH CAROLINA

Batesburg-Leesville School
Margaret N. Camp
School Counselor
121 West Columbia Avenue
Batesburg, SC 29006
(803) 532-4452

Windsor Elementary School
Trish Ruhle
School Counselor
2839 Hobkirk Rd.
Columbia, SC 29223
(803) 788-1783

Chapin Elementary School
Patricia S. Gaddis
School Counselor
940 Old Bush River Road
Chapin, SC 29036
(803) 345-2214

Nursery Road Elementary School
Margaret H. Jennings
School Counselor
6706 Nursery Road
Columbia, SC 29212
(803) 781-8770

Forest Lake Elementary School
Ron Miles
School Counselor
6801 Brookfield Road
Columbia, SC 29206
(803) 782-0470

Seven Oaks Elementary School
Lynda Neese
School Counselor
2800 Ashland Road
Columbia, SC 29210
(803) 798-6500

South Carolina *Continued*

Joseph Keels Elementary School
Tommie C. Toner
School Counselor
7801 Springview Street
Columbia, SC 29223
(803) 788-5420

Irmo Elementary School
Diane S. Senn
School Counselor
7401 Gibbes Street
Irmo, SC 29063
(803) 781-2626

SOUTH DAKOTA

Sioux Falls Instructional Planning
    Center
Jerry Mayer
Supervisor of Guidance and
    Counseling
201 E. 38th Street
Sioux Falls, SD 57117
(605) 331-7927

Sioux Falls Public Schools
Cathy LeDuc
School Counselor
4501 S. Holbrook
Sioux Falls, SD 57106
(605) 361-8956

TENNESSEE

Memphis City Schools
Faye C. Deanes
Supervisor of Guidance and
    Counseling
2597 Avery Avenue
Memphis, TN 38112
(901) 454-5228

Memphis City Schools
W.W. Davis
Director of Attendance and
    Guidance
2597 Avery Avenue
Memphis, TN 38112
(901) 454-5228

Memphis City Schools
Susan James
Director of Parenting Center of
    Memphis
499 Patterson Street
Memphis, TN 38111
(901) 452-3830

TEXAS

Arlington Schools
Reba Sommerville
Coordinator of Testing and
    Elementary Guidance
1203 West Pioneer Parkway
Arlington, TX 76016
(817) 459-7322

Goose Creek Consolidated
    Independent School District
Mike Madison
Deputy Superintendent of Schools
P.O. Box 30
Baytown, TX 77522
(713) 428-2553

Irving Independent School District
Rebecca Downing
Supervisor of Counseling
901 N. O'Connor Road
Irving, TX 75061
(214) 259-4575

Katy Independent School District
Jan Shivers
Consultant
Student Services
6301 S. Stadium Lane
Katy, TX 77450
(713) 391-2184

Richardson Independent School
   District
Lynn Caldwell
Consultant
Guidance and Counseling
400 S. Greenville Avenue
Richardson, TX 75081
(214) 238-8111

Northside Independent School
   District
Patricia Henderson
Director of Guidance
5900 Evers Road
San Antonio, TX 78238
(512) 647-2218

UTAH

Jordan School District
Family Educational Center
Fulvia Nicholson
Counselor
8449 South 150 West
Midvale, UT
(801) 565-7442

VERMONT

Shelburne Village School
Sally Lamphier
School Counselor
RD 4, Box 69
Shelburne, VT 05482
(802) 985-2541

Shelburne School District Guidance
   Program
Charles Cerasoli
Supervisor of Guidance and
   Counseling
Harbor Road
Shelburne, VT 05482
(802) 985-3331

Browns River Middle School
   Guidance Program
Debra Chisholm
School Counselor
RR#1, Box 3345
Underhill, VT 05489
(802) 899-3711, 3670

VIRGINIA

Amherst County Schools
Evelyn H. Woodruff
Elementary Supervisor
P.O. Box 1257
Amherst, VA 24521
(804) 929-6931

Harrisonburg City Schools
Marian J. Stickley
Director of Instruction
317 S. Main Street
Harrisonburg, VA 22801
(703) 434-9916

Willard Model School
Pamela Kloeppel
Director of Guidance
800 E. City Hall Avenue
Norfolk, VA 23501
(804) 441-2640

Henrico County Schools
Adams Elementary School
Amanda Spencer
School Counselor
600 S. Laburnum Avenue
Richmond, VA 23223
(804) 222-1437

Virginia *Continued*

Roanoke County Schools
Gary L. Kelly
Supervisor of Guidance and
   Curriculum Coordination
526 College Avenue
Salem, VA 24153
(703) 387-6416

Staunton City Schools
Ferraba W. Whitesell
Elementary Supervisor
503 DuPont Avenue
Staunton, VA 24401
(703) 885-0354

Rawls Byrd School
Mickie Meyer
School Counselor
112 Laurel Lane
Williamsburg, VA 23185
(804) 229-7597

Matthew Whaley Primary School
Loretta Kreps
School Counselor
Scotland Street
Williamsburg, VA 23185
(804) 229-1931

Norge Primary School
Gary Waynick
School Counselor
7311 Richmond Road
Williamsburg, VA 23185
(804) 564-3372

WASHINGTON

Spring Glen Elementary School
Ralph O. Jones
School Counselor
2607 Jones Avenue South
Renton, WA 98055
(206) 859-7494, 95

WEST VIRGINIA

Boone County Public Schools
Project PAL (Providing Assistance for
   Learning)
David Sabatino
Supervisor
c/o West Virginia College of
   Graduate Studies
Institute, WV 25112
(304) 768-9711

Anna Jarvis Elementary School
Bob Rubenstein
School Counselor
Grafton, WV 26354
(304) 265-4090

East Park Elementary/Middle School
Dolores Gaskin
School Counselor
1025 Fairfax
Fairmont, WV 26554
(304) 363-0660

WISCONSIN

Appleton Area School District
Christine Muir
School Counselor
P.O. Box 2019
Appleton, WI 54913
(414) 735-6161

Cleveland Heights Elementary
   School
Delma Erikson
School Counselor
16401 W. Cleveland Ave.
New Berlin, WI 53151
(414) 782-5515

Eau Claire Area School District
James R. Jacobs
Asst. Director of Special Services
500 Main Street
Eau Claire, WI 54701
(715) 833-3471

Menasha School District
Ron Stark
School Counselor
449 Ahnaip Street
Menasha, WI 54952
(414) 729-5070

Racine Unified School District
Donna Tartagni
Director of Guidance
2220 Northwestern Avenue
Racine, WI 53404
(414) 631-7092

Rhinelander School District
Cheryl Hanson
School Counselor
315 S. Oneida Avenue
Rhinelander, WI 54501
(715) 362-4990

Sheboygan Area School District
Jefferson Elementary School
Cheryl Hedgecock
School Counselor
1538 N. 15th Street
Sheboygan, WI 53081
(414) 459-3620

Sturgeon Bay Public Schools
Shirley Senarighi
School Counselor
1230 Michigan Street
Sturgeon Bay, WI 54235
(414) 743-6511

Waukesha School District
Sandra Bosin
Guidance Coordinator
2744 Minot Lane
Waukesha, WI 53186
(414) 521-8844

Waunakee Elementary School
Douglas P. Green
School Counselor
501 South Street
Waunakee, WI 53597
(608) 849-8191

WYOMING

Converse County School District #1
East Elementary School
William L. McKay
School Counselor
P.O. Box 1028
Douglas, WY 82633
(307) 358-3502

Converse County School District #2
Grant Elementary School
Sharon E. Larson
School Counselor
Glenrock, WY 82637
(307) 436-2774

Sweetwater County School District
  #1
Yellowstone Elementary School
Vicky Swartz
School Counselor
P.O. Box 1089
Rocksprings, WY 82901
(307) 362-1289

FIGURES AND FORMS

FIGURE 1

NOMINATION FORM

EXEMPLARY ELEMENTARY COUNSELING PROGRAM

Location of Program: _____

Name of Contact Person: _____

Address: _____

_____

Phone No.: _____

What is the primary focus of this program (e.g., parent education, group counseling)?

_____

_____

Describe the strengths and exemplary features of this program.

_____

_____

_____

_____

Your Name: _____

Title: _____

Address: _____

_____

Phone No.: _____

FIGURE 2

EXEMPLARY ELEMENTARY PROGRAMS AND PRACTICES QUESTIONNAIRE

Name of Respondent _____

School Address _____

City _____ State _____ Zip _____

Daytime Telephone   Area Code (___) Number _____

Name of Program _____

Target Group Served _____

Current Position
Elementary school counselor 1
Elementary supervisor of guidance and counseling 2
Other (specify) _____ 3

Is your assignment full-time?
Yes 1
No 2

Number of schools to which you are assigned or for which you are responsible _____

_____

Approximate student/counselor ratio _____

1. Some people have described the primary objectives of their counseling program in the following manner:

   . . . individual counseling, small group counseling, classroom guidance and parent involvement
   . . . elementary service teams related to assessing and meeting student needs
   . . . responsive services to children with special needs

   The primary objectives of our elementary counseling program are:

   _____
   _____
   _____
   _____
   _____
   _____
   _____
   _____
   _____

2. Some people have described the major strengths and exemplary features of their program as follows:

   . . . we have a sequential classroom guidance curriculum
   . . . we have an excellent staffing pattern—one counselor for 250 students
   . . . the team approach with teachers, health services, administrators

The major strengths and exemplary features of our elementary counseling program are:

_____

_____

_____

_____

_____

_____

3. Some people have identified specific innovative, unusual, or highly effective practices or approaches as:

   . . . peer helpers—selected 6th-grade students are taught special helping techniques
   . . . career club—members research various careers and make presentations about careers
   . . . we have the "choosy chewers" group, a group for overweight youngsters

The specific innovative, unusual, or highly effective practices or approaches in our program are:

_____

_____

_____

_____

_____

_____

_____

_____

4. Indicate below any other features of your program that make it noteworthy and exemplary. (Include such areas as evaluation, special recognition, materials, additional resources.)

\
\
\
\
\
\
\
\
\
\
\

5. Has your program received special recognition other than this nomination? Describe.

\
\

6. Are there special materials used in your program? Describe.

\
\

7. Are there additional school resources or staff used in your program? Describe.

\
\

8. Do you use any community resources in your program? Describe.

\
\

9. Have you had to overcome any major obstacles in conducting your program? Describe.

\
\

10. Is this exemplary program part of the regular elementary guidance program?
     Yes 1
     No 2

     Describe. _____

     _____

     _____

     _____

11. Length of time program has been operating:
     One year or less 1
     Two to four years 2
     More than four years 3

12. Primary financial support for this program comes from:
     Regular district budget 1
     Additional funding 2
     Other (specify) _____ 3

13. Number of elementary schools participating in this exemplary program:
     One school 1
     More than one school 2
          Total number: _____

14. Total number of students participating in this exemplary program:
     Fewer than 100 1
     Between 100 and 300 2
     Between 301 and 500 3
     Between 501 and 700 4
     Between 701 and 900 5
     More than 900 6

15. What are the grade levels in school(s) with exemplary program (e.g., K–5)? _____

     _____

16. Type of community:
     Urban 1
     Suburban 2
     Rural 3
     Other (specify _____ 4

17. Socioeconomic status of students:
     Primarily upper-middle class 1
     Primarily middle-class 2
     Primarily working-class 3
     Primarily inner-city 4
     Other (specify) _____ 5

18. Racial/ethnic background of students:
    Predominantly White 1
    Predominantly Black 2
    Predominantly Hispanic 3
    Other (specify) —————————————————————————— 4

PLEASE COMPLETE THE FOLLOWING QUESTIONS FOR STATISTICAL PURPOSES

19. Age:
    Under 30 1
    31 to 40 2
    41 to 50 3
    Over 50 4

20. Sex:
    Female 1
    Male 2

21. Marital status:
    Married 1
    Not married 2

22. Racial/ethnic background:
    Black 1
    Ilispanic 2
    White 3
    Other (specify) —————————————————————————— 4

23. Current degree status:
    Bachelor's 1
    Master's 2
    Education specialist 3
    Doctorate 4

24. Do you have certification or endorsement as a school counselor?
    Yes 1
        Year obtained: ——————————
    No 2

25. What other certifications or licenses do you hold? Circle all that apply.
    NCC 1
    State license as professional counselor 2
    State license as psychologist 3
    Other (specify) _____ 4
    None 5

26. How many years have you been working as an elementary school counselor or
    supervisor?
    Fewer than 3 1
    3 to 10 2
    More than 10 3

FIGURE 3

ABSTRACTED CONFERENCE PROGRAM

*Exemplary Programs and Practices
in Elementary School Counseling*

May 12 & 13, 1988

Virginia Tech
Donaldson Brown Center for Continuing Education
Blacksburg, Virginia

Sponsored by
Christa McAuliffe Fellowship Program
U.S. Department of Education
Virginia Department of Education
Virginia Tech
Craig County Virginia Public Schools

MAJOR SESSION PRESENTERS

Robert D. Myrick of the University of Florida is a nationally acclaimed expert on elementary school counseling. Dr. Myrick has written extensively in the area of elementary school guidance and counseling and is a consultant to many school districts in planning new programs.

Libby Hoffman is Supervisor of Elementary School Guidance and Counseling at the Virginia Department of Education. Dr. Hoffman is a graduate of the University of Virginia and has been at the forefront of the elementary school guidance and counseling movement in the Commonwealth for 10 years. She has been instrumental in providing the leadership that resulted in a mandate to include counseling in all elementary schools in the state.

Kathleen Nininger is the elementary school counselor and *Martha Blount* is the elementary school principal at Back Creek and Bent Mountain Elementary Schools in Roanoke County, Virginia. Dr. Nininger and Ms. Blount have worked together and established a highly effective and successful elementary school counseling program that has become an invaluable asset to their schools and community.

CONCURRENT SESSION PRESENTERS

WYNNE INTERMEDIATE SCHOOL, Wynne, Arkansas
Presenter: Sue Hull, School Counselor

This presentation will provide an overview of some developmental classroom guidance programs used in grades three through five. Discussion will include practices such as Student Host Program (peer training to assist new students), the Safety Kids Club, and "Where Do I Belong?" (a divorce support group for students). A list of materials will be provided.

Special Recognitions/Awards
1985 Arkansas Elementary School Counselor of Year
President-elect, Arkansas School Counselor Association

PINAR ELEMENTARY SCHOOL, Orange County, Florida
Presenter: Nancy Allen, School Counselor

The Guidance Program from Pinar Elementary School, Orlando, Florida, will be presented in two parts. First, there will be a slide presentation, with commentary, depicting the various aspects of the program. Second, a booklet providing more detailed information will be distributed to each participant. At the end of the session, questions will be encouraged from the audience.

Special Recognitions/Awards
Co-author: *Guidance Activities for the Elementary School, Guide for Elementary Counselors in Career Counseling*, and *IMPACT: Guidance Lessons for Middle Schools*

HAILMAN ELEMENTARY/CRICHFIELD ELEMENTARY SCHOOLS, La Porte, Indiana
Presenter: Sally Mayes, School Counselor

This presentation will highlight a typical day in the life of an elementary school counselor. Examples of classroom guidance and small group guidance will be presented. The session will also feature "How to Schedule Your Counseling Day!"

Special Recognitions/Awards
1988 Indiana Counselor of the Year

EAST BATON ROUGE PARISH SCHOOL DISTRICT, Baton Rouge, Louisiana
Presenter: Betty Addison, Supervisor of Elementary Guidance

Elementary Guidance—Baton Rouge Style—is developmental, preventive in scope (not crisis oriented, though this too is a part of our work). This presentation is directed toward activities and techniques used with students every day, i.e. decision-making skills, healthy self-image and a sense of responsibility in the pursuit of academic achievement and personal development.

FORT RIVER ELEMENTARY SCHOOL, Amherst, Massachusetts
Presenter: Mary Ivey, School Counselor

The Fort River program is a development program serving multilevel populations. Special features of the program will be presented including individual and group counseling, program development, consultation with teachers and staff, work with parents and the community, training other counselors and teachers in the area, and participation in writing and sharing the ideas of microcounseling and developmental counseling with the profession at large. Video tape examples of developmental counseling will be shown.

Special Recognition/Awards
Merit Counselor—1986—Recognized for excellence in the Amherst School System
Award from North Atlantic Region, Association for Counselor Education and Supervision convention as best program presented, 1985.

JEFFERSON ELEMENTARY SCHOOL, Rochester, Minnesota
Presenters: Jane Bogan, School Counselor, and Kathy Estry, Guidance Committee Chairperson

This presentation is an overview of a successful school-wide effort to address the affective needs of children through a developmental guidance program initiated four years ago. You will be provided with practical strategies for planning, implementing, and evaluating your emerging program. Materials and a bibliography of resources will be available.

Special Recognition/Awards
Recipient of 1987–88 Minnesota School of Excellence Award
Principal was chosen as 1987–88 Outstanding Minnesota School Counselor Administrator

FOREST LAKE ELEMENTARY SCHOOL, Columbia, South Carolina
Presenter: Ron Miles, School Counselor

Where Do I Begin? This presentation will focus on practical and field tested approaches for planning, implementing, and evaluating a developmental elementary guidance and counseling program. A three year program module will be presented. The following areas will be addressed: surveying community needs, effective public relations, classroom guidance, small group guidance and counseling, parenting education, designing a guidance office and establishing power in the work setting.

Special Recognition/Awards
South Carolina Elementary Counselor of the Year, 1988
Teacher of the Year, Forest Lake Elementary School, 1988
Outstanding Columbia Area Educator, 1983

NORTHSIDE INDEPENDENT SCHOOL DISTRICT, San Antonio, Texas
Presenter, Pat Henderson, Director of Guidance

This presentation will address developmental elementary school guidance and counseling from a division-wide perspective. The focus will be on preventive measures within a comprehensive K–12 guidance program. Elementary components will be emphasized and the elementary counselor job description will be shared.

ROANOKE COUNTY PUBLIC SCHOOLS, Salem, Virginia
Presenters: Gary Kelly, Supervisor of Guidance; Kathleen Nininger, School Counselor; Treva Richter, School Counselor; Jackie Turman, School Counselor; Jane Fralin, School Counselor; Joanne Lehman, School Counselor

The framework for a comprehensive 15-year-old developmental counseling program will be presented. It exhibits a collaborative effort utilizing diversified personalities unified through counseling objectives based on identified student needs. This program is exemplified by the collective effort and support of administration, staff, parents, and community.

EAU CLAIRE AREA SCHOOL DISTRICT, Eau Claire, Wisconsin
Presenters: James Jacobs, Supervisor of Elementary Guidance; Sonja Stoudt, School Counselor; Ilene Doty, School Counselor

The Eau Claire presentation will give an overview of the system-wide program with emphasis on goals and objectives and how they are achieved. The presentation will feature a slide presentation plus discussion of the overall program and how it is adapted and implemented in the individual schools of the district.

MEMBERS OF BLUE RIBBON SELECTION COMMITTEE

Mary E. Gehrke, Elementary Counselor, Racine, Wisconsin, Vice President for Elementary, American School Counselor Association

Edwin R. Gerler, Jr., Associate Professor of Counselor Education, North Carolina State University, Raleigh, North Carolina

Martin Gerstein, Associate Professor of Counselor Education, Virginia Polytechnic Institute and State University, Blacksburg, Virginia

Catherine Gordon, Elementary Counselor, retired, Edgewater, Maryland

Mary Joe Hannaford, Supervisor of Guidance, retired, Gwinette County, Dunwoody, Georgia

William Henry, Principal, Smith Elementary School, Dayton, Ohio, (Nominated by National Association of Elementary School Principals)

Libby Hoffman, Supervisor of Elementary School Guidance and Counseling, Virginia Department of Education

Marilyn Hutchins, Advanced doctoral student in elementary counseling, Virginia Polytechnic Institute and State University, Blacksburg, Virginia

Marilyn Lichtman, Associate Professor of Research, Virginia Polytechnic Institute and State University, Blacksburg, Virginia

Sue Mihalik, Chief Guidance Consultant, Texas Department of Education

Robert D. Myrick, Professor of Counselor Education, University of Florida, Gainesville, Florida

Stewart D. Roberson, Principal, Walker-Grant Intermediate School, Fredericksburg, Virginia

Shirley Woodall, Christa McAuliffe Research Fellow, Craig County Public Schools, Craig County, Virginia

Arlene Zielke, Parent representative, Chicago, Illinois, Nominated by National Parent Teachers Association

FIGURE 4

FIRST ROUND RATING FORM

Name of Rater _____

1. First Round Rating

Instructions: Rate each program. Write the number of your rating in the space provided below. Return the rating sheet to us by <u>February 15</u>.

THIS PROGRAM IS AMONG THE BEST OF THIS GROUP OF PROGRAMS IN TERMS OF OBJECTIVES, STRENGTHS, EXEMPLARY FEATURES, OR INNOVATIVE, UNUSUAL, OR HIGHLY EFFECTIVE PRACTICES.

STRONGLY AGREE	AGREE	DISAGREE	STRONGLY DISAGREE
1	2	3	4

Code	Your Rating	Code	Your Rating	Code	Your Rating
101		135		169	
103		137		171	
105		139		173	
107		141		175	
109		143		177	
111		145		179	
113		147		181	
115		149		183	
117		151		185	
119		153		187	
121		155		189	
123		157		191	
125		159		193	
127		161		195	
129		163		197	
131		165		199	
133		167		201	

FIGURE 5

RATING FORM

Name of Rater _____

2. Summary of First Round Ratings and Second Round Ratings.

Instructions: Examine the average ratings for each program. Compare your ratings (individual ratings have been provided) with the average ratings. Revise your ratings (if desired) and put your responses in the appropriate column. Return the rating sheet to us by February 26, 1988.

> THIS PROGRAM IS AMONG THE BEST OF THIS GROUP OF PROGRAMS IN TERMS OF OBJECTIVES, STRENGTHS, EXEMPLARY FEATURES, OR INNOVATIVE, UNUSUAL, OR HIGHLY EFFECTIVE PRACTICES.
>
> | STRONGLY AGREE | AGREE | DISAGREE | STRONGLY DISAGREE |
> |:---:|:---:|:---:|:---:|
> | 1 | 2 | 3 | 4 |

Code	Your Orig. Rating	Avg.	Your Revised Rating	Code	Your Orig. Rating	Avg.	Your Revised Rating	Code	Your Orig. Rating	Avg.	Your Revised Rating
101		2.0		135		1.5		169		1.8	
103		3.9		137		2.3		171		1.4	
105		1.1		139		2.4		173		2.8	
107		2.0		141		3.8		175		2.6	
109		2.1		143		2.5		177		2.1	
111		omit		145		2.3		179		2.5	
113		3.0		147		1.8		181		2.1	
115		2.1		149		2.1		183		1.9	
117		1.9		151		1.8		185		1.4	
119		2.4		153		2.6		187		omit	
121		2.1		155		2.9		189		1.8	
123		1.6		157		omit		191		1.6	
125		1.6		159		1.9		193		2.5	
127		omit		161		2.0		195		1.6	
129		2.8		163		2.4		197		1.9	
131		1.8		165		omit		199		1.6	
133		2.6		167		2.3		201		2.6	

FIGURE 6

EXEMPLARY ELEMENTARY SCHOOL COUNSELING PROGRAMS
EVALUATION OF CONFERENCE

We are interested in your opinions about this conference. Please take a few minutes to complete this questionnaire. Return it to the designated locations when you leave. Thank you for your help.

1. Overall rating of the conference	Excellent	Good	Fair	Poor
2. Quality of presentations	Excellent	Good	Fair	Poor
3. Usefulness of information	Excellent	Good	Fair	Poor
4. Applicability for your needs	Excellent	Good	Fair	Poor
5. Effectiveness of presenters	Excellent	Good	Fair	Poor

BELOW ARE SOME WORDS AND PHRASES THAT MIGHT BE USED TO DESCRIBE CONFERENCES. INDICATE THE EXTENT TO WHICH <u>YOU THINK</u> THESE STATEMENTS APPLY TO THIS CONFERENCE.

	Considerably	Usually	Somewhat	Not Very
6. Challenging	____	____	____	____
7. Innovative	____	____	____	____
8. Educational	____	____	____	____
9. Entertaining	____	____	____	____
10. Boring	____	____	____	____
11. Timely	____	____	____	____
12. Important	____	____	____	____
13. Thought-provoking	____	____	____	____
14. Controversial	____	____	____	____
15. Unfocused	____	____	____	____
16. Exciting	____	____	____	____
17. Needed	____	____	____	____

18. Current Position:
Elementary School Counselor .... ____
Teacher .... ____
Principal .... ____
Director or Supervisor of Guidance/Counseling/Pupil Personnel .... ____
College Professor .... ____
State Level or Central Office Administrator .... ____
Other _____

19. Number of years in this position: .... ____

20. Currently studying to be a counselor?   ____Yes   ____No

21. Status of elementary counseling in your school division:
    No plans for counselors .... _____
    Do not have any, but expect to within 1–2 years .... _____
    Have counselors in some schools, but not required .... _____
    Counselors required in schools .... _____
    Not connected with school division .... _____
    Other _____
22. Were you on the program of this conference?   _____ Yes   _____ No
23. What state are you from? _____
24. Would you attend a conference next year?   _____ Yes   _____ No
25. What topics do you believe should be covered in future conferences?

    _____

    _____